C

# ATLAS OF THE ENVIRONMENT

**Editor:** Roger Coote
**Designer:** Ross George
**Cartography:** Swanston Graphics Ltd

First published in 1991 by
Wayland (Publishers) Ltd
61 Western Road, Hove
East Sussex BN3 1JD, England

© Copyright 1991 Wayland (Publishers) Ltd

**British Library Cataloguing in Publication Data**
Atlas of the environment.
 I. Baines, John
 333 . 7

ISBN  0  7502 0200 9

Typeset by Ross George
Printed by Rotolito Lombarda S. p. A., Milan
Bound by Casterman S. A., Belgium

## Picture Acknowledgements

The publishers would like to thank the following for allowing their pictures to be reproduced in this book:
Bruce Coleman Ltd front cover right (Michael Fogden), 8 (John Cancalosi), 11 (Leonard Lee Rue III), 21 (Alain Compost), 25 (Michael Fogden), 27 bottom (N.G. Blake), 30-31 (Hans Reinhard), 34 (Gerald Cubitt), 34-5 (Nicholas Devore), 39 bottom (Udo Hirsch), 41 (Henneghien), 45 (Peter Davey), 52-3 (Hans-Peter Merten), 60-61 (Robert P. Carr), 75 (N.G. Blake), 81 (C. James), 86 (Chris James), 87 bottom (J. Cancalosi); Frank Lane 10 (C. Carvalho), 27 top (Derek Hall), 47 bottom (Jean Hosking); Greenpeace 67 (Edwards), 69 (Walker), 90 (Perez); Hutchison Library 28-9, 31, 36, 62, 72-3 (Michael Macintyre), 76; ICCE front cover left (John Parrott), 83 top (Mark Boulton), 84 (Rob Cousins); ICI Fibres 50; Miriam Moss 83 bottom; Oxford Scientific Films front cover centre (Frank Huber), 9 (Michael Fogden), 13 (Doug Allan), 29 (Richard Kolar/Earth Scenes), 36-7 (Tim Shepherd), 50-51 (John McCammon), 59 top (Lena Beyer), 68 (Kim Westerskov), 89 (Stan Osolinski); Panos Pictures 4 (Ron Giling),12 top (Alain Le Garsmeur), 16-17 (Paul Harrison), 18-19 (Ron Giling), 19 (Ron Giling), 20 (Ron Giling), 26 (Michael Harvey), 39 top (Ron Giling), 43 (Ron Giling), 44-5 (Bruce Paton), 63 (Jeremy Hartley); Papilio 73; Planet Earth Pictures 8-9 (J. Scott), 12 bottom (Peter David), 24 Richard Beales), 47 top (John Lythgoe), 53 (Brian Coope), 62-3 (J. Bracegirdle), 91 (Nigel Merrett); Topham Picture Source 35 (Hans Silvester/Rapho), 54 (Associated Press), 70 (Associated Press), 70-71 (Associated Press), 76-7 (Associated Press), 77 (Associated Press), 78-9 (Associated Press), 80 (Associated Press); Wayland Picture Library  55, 59 bottom, 66-7; Zefa 15 (Justitz), 57 (Bob Croxford), 79  (Davies), 87 top (Griffith). All maps and diagrams are by Swanston Graphics Ltd. Front cover artwork is by Peter Bull.

## LIST OF CONTRIBUTORS

INTRODUCTION – **John Howson** is education officer for the environmental organization Friends of the Earth.

THE NATURAL WORLD – **Andrew Kelly** is an environmentalist, and a writer and editor of books for children. He lives and works in Victoria, Australia.

THE HUMAN WORLD – **Stephen Sterling** is a researcher, writer and lecturer on environmental matters, and a consultant in environmental education.

FALLING FORESTS – **Liz Chidley**, formerly of the World Wide Fund for Nature, now works as a freelance researcher and writer.

FOOD AND FARMING – **Hannah Pearce** trained as an environmentalist and later worked for Friends of the Earth. She is now a freelance journalist.

DESERTIFICATION – **Dr Ewan McLeish** is the director of the Council for Environmental Education. He has written widely on environmental issues, and is the author of *The Spread of Deserts* in Wayland's 'Conserving Our World' series.

ENERGY CRISIS – **Damian Randle**, formerly education officer at the Centre for Alternative Technology in Machnylleth, Wales, is now the editor of *Green Teacher* magazine. He is also a freelance writer and researcher.

AIR POLLUTION – **John Baines** is an ex-teacher and former director of the Council for Environmental Education. He is a well-known freelance writer and researcher, and is the author of *Protecting the Oceans* and *Acid Rain* in Wayland's 'Conserving Our World' series.

POLLUTED WATERS – **Dr René Heijnis**, who lives in Zaandam, the Netherlands, is a specialist in environmental biology and ecology. He has been a member of the Examination Group of the Dutch Department of Education, and is the author of a number of educational books and information packs.

CLIMATE UNDER THREAT – **Robert Harris** worked in Africa for several years, and has written for the United Nations Council of Refugees in Nairobi, and for the Canadian International Development Agency. He now lives in Canada where he is a library consultant and works on schools environmental projects for an educational publisher.

CONSERVING OUR WORLD – **Barbara James** works for the Council for Environmental Education and is also a freelance writer and researcher on environmental issues. She is the author of *Waste and Recycling* and *Conserving the Polar Regions* in Wayland's 'Conserving Our World' series.

Consultant – **Colin Harris** is the Adviser on Environmental Education for Hertfordshire County Council, and an executive member of the Environmental Education Advisers Association.

# CONTENTS

Where does the environment start and where does it end? This is one of those questions that has no answer. After all, we are talking about the whole biosphere – perhaps the whole universe. Everything is a part of the environment. Albert Einstein, the founder of modern nuclear physics, once said that the environment is everything that isn't me; these days it would include him, too.

So an atlas of the environment is a very good way of looking at problems that affect the whole globe.

One important message of this atlas is that, in environmental terms as well as in economic terms, it is the developing world that suffers most. Not only do most poor developing countries owe the rich, developed nations a lot of money, but they are often forced to damage their environment in trying to pay it back.

Whether it be for making such things as door handles or mahogany toilet seats, the cost is some of the richest habitats on earth, and possibly the extinction of some of the earth's unique species of plant or animal. Perhaps one of the most urgent problems facing the earth is to help these nations develop their economies in a way that is good for local communities and does not harm the environment.

Many of the world's surviving tribal peoples, such as the Penans in Malaysia – one of the few who still live by hunting and gathering – are also under threat from the loss of the forests which are their home.

If we were to take a journey into space from the earth's surface, we would first of all see the environment in the way we see it every day – the city streets and traffic jams, and the huge fields growing, perhaps, a single crop. As we got further away we could view a district or even a whole country. We would see the polluted oceans, the huge wheat prairies, the sprawling cities, and the connecting motorways cutting deep scars through natural habitats.

From far out in space we could look back and see some of the massive problems that face the earth today, such as the hacking down of the forests and, if we had a special camera, ozone depletion over the polar regions.

We may even see the smogs generated by our cities, the spreading deserts and the lines made by our roads – just some of the evidence of human activity.

Finally we would see a small globe – our planet. We would be looking at a single earth, without boundaries or zones. Perhaps we need to keep all these different views in our minds if we are to realize that environmental problems are linked to one another, and to understand how we can start to put things right.

Although the scale of the problems seems huge, it is vital to remember that we all have an important role to play in safeguarding the planet's future – not just how we can benefit the environment by what we do, but also in the influence we have on others. It is actions such as those of women in rural India, who have encouraged tree-planting in their community, that show us a way forward. Your own school can play its part by recycling paper, saving energy, or encouraging wildlife.

The best time to begin improving the environment is now, and this atlas is a good place to start. It is full of information to help you understand the problems affecting the world we live in, and about how you can help. When you have read it, you might want to become involved with an organization – such as Friends of the Earth – which is fighting to help protect the environment.

The atlas's view of the planet focuses on a range of environmental issues, such as the destruction of habitats, energy use, and air and water pollution. It shows how they are caused and the ways in which the problems are related. For instance, air pollution is connected with transport issues and the way we use energy. Climate change is being brought about by the way in which we produce our energy, and other issues such as transport and the destruction of tropical forests.

In the end, both the problems and their solutions depend upon how we look at the earth and the way we fit into it. We need to realize that we are actually a part of the natural world, and that it is not there just for our convenience or for us to destroy.

**Left** *Many developing countries cannot afford to spend money on protecting the environment.*

**John Howson**
**Education Officer, Friends of the Earth**

# THE NATURAL WORLD

Of all the planets in our solar system, life exists only on earth. The surface of Mercury, for example, is far too hot for life to survive, while that of Pluto is far too cold. Only earth has water and an atmosphere to nourish and protect life, and only earth sustains the narrow band of temperatures in which life can thrive.

Life on earth is almost unbelievably varied in its abundance of odd, grotesque and beautiful forms. There is scarcely a place on the planet that is not inhabited by some living creature. There are bacteria that can live in the petrol tanks of jet planes, and insects that survive in springs that reach 50°C. The young of brine fly live in almost pure salt, and there are worms that live under the eyelids of hippopotamuses and feed only on their tears. Even in the ice and rocks high above the permanent snow-line in the Himalayas, life survives in the form of small insects.

*The different climates and landforms of the earth determine where different sorts of vegetation will occur. Types of vegetation are grouped into communities which scientists call biomes. This map shows the earth's main biomes.*

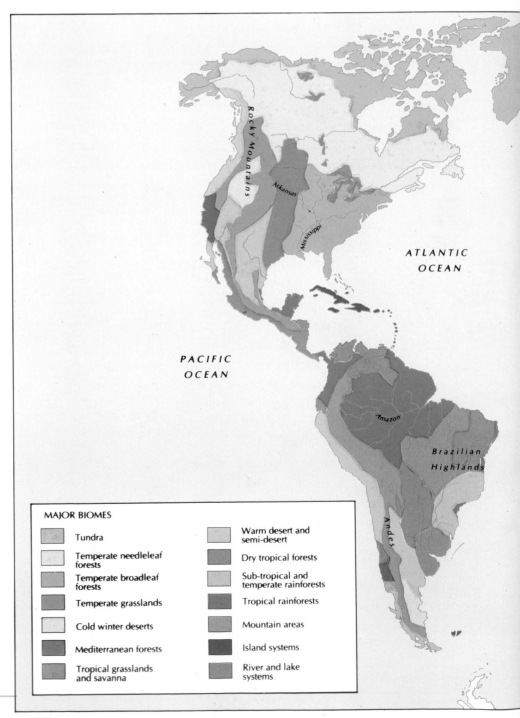

MAJOR BIOMES

- Tundra
- Temperate needleleaf forests
- Temperate broadleaf forests
- Temperate grasslands
- Cold winter deserts
- Mediterranean forests
- Tropical grasslands and savanna
- Warm desert and semi-desert
- Dry tropical forests
- Sub-tropical and temperate rainforests
- Tropical rainforests
- Mountain areas
- Island systems
- River and lake systems

There may be as many as 8 million different species of plants and animals on earth, most of which are still unknown to science. A handful of soil may contain more than a million species of bacteria, as well as 100,000 yeast cells and 50,000 species of fungus. A hectare of rich farming soil could contain as many as 300 million small invertebrate creatures, such as mites and millipedes. This teeming multitude of life, among which we humans are just one species, exists in a thin layer around the outside of the earth, that scientists call the biosphere.

## The biosphere

The biosphere is the layer of soil, air and water in which animals and plants live and die. Although earth is one of the smaller planets in the solar system, it is 6,300 kilometres from the surface to the centre.

Most of the planet consists of the rocks of the mantle and core, much of which are molten. At 100 kilometres beneath the surface, the temperature is 3,000°C, far too hot for anything to live.

The atmosphere is estimated to extend 200 kilometres from the earth's surface, but beyond about 30 kilometres it is far too cold for any form of life to survive.

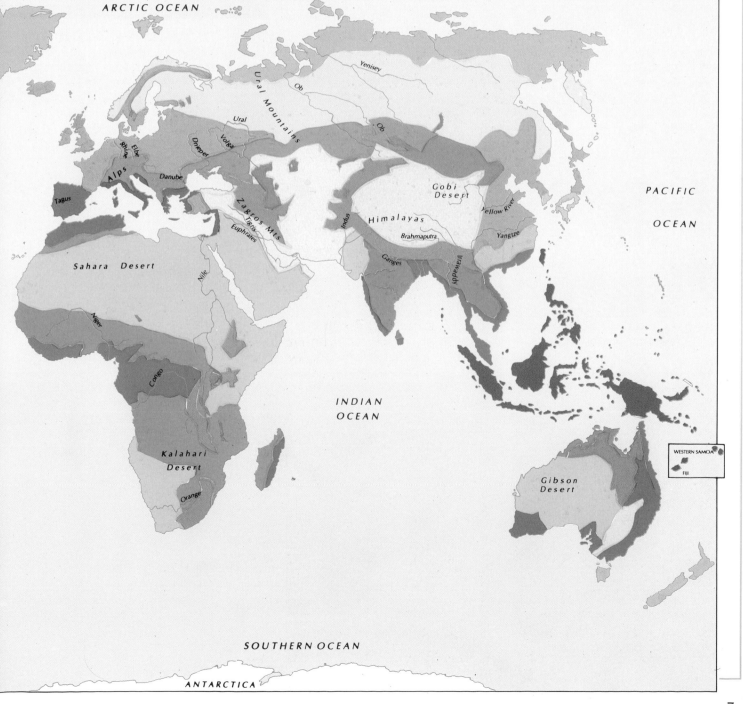

## Where did life come from?

Life began on earth around 3.8 billion years ago. Very simple single-celled organisms, similar to bacteria, developed in the warm seas which then covered the planet. Over billions of years these organisms lived, produced new organisms and died. Slowly they evolved into the enormously complex and diverse system that we know today.

Evolution is the process through which this rich diversity of life has developed. New organisms have been produced through the processes of natural selection and adaptation.

Throughout the history of the earth the environment has been constantly, if slowly, changing. Life has adapted to these changes, producing many different forms. Successful forms of life survived and produced more offspring; less successful forms became extinct, or died out.

Very gradually life became more complicated and diverse. Since life began, many more species have died out than exist in the world today.

### The Serengeti

An example of a superbly rich and beautiful ecosystem is the savannah lands that form the Serengeti Plains in Africa. More than half a million animals live on the Serengeti. The savannah teems with life and each species uses a different part of the environment for food. The giraffe with its long neck browses in the tops of the trees. The eland can stand on its hind legs to reach the leaves at the middle level. Smaller species of antelope browse on the lower branches, while the springbok grazes on the grass around the foot of the trees and the warthog unearths roots.

*The sun sets over the Serengeti Plains in Africa.*

For hundreds of millions of years, life existed only in the sea. Primitive forms of sea urchins, worms, molluscs and sponges lived in the forests of seaweed. Plants did not appear on land until 400 million years ago. When the first plants began to emerge from the sea and colonize the land, simple animals like the worms followed. Other, more complex, animals followed later and eventually evolved into the many different forms of reptiles and amphibians that dominated the earth during the age of dinosaurs. The dinosaurs died out about 70 million years ago, at about the same time that mammals appeared.

The atmosphere of the earth is quite unlike that of other planets. As life evolved, the earth evolved with it. Living organisms released oxygen into the atmosphere, which altered the balance of atmospheric gases and made survival possible.

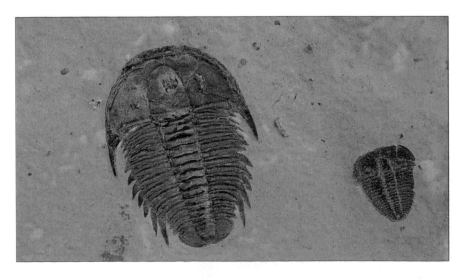

**Left** *About 600 million years ago, creatures like this fossilized trilobite were common in the seas on earth.*

**Below** *The Grand Canyon in the USA has been created over a period of millions of years by the Colorado River wearing away the rocks over which it flows.*

## Ecology

As organisms evolved they interacted with the world around them and with each other to form complex, inter-dependent ecosystems. All forms of life are inter-dependent; none can exist in isolation. For example, many animals depend on plants for food and many plants depend on animals to pollinate their flowers. These relationships can become very close and quite complex, as in the case of the ant acacia, a kind of tree that lives in the tropics. Ant acacias have developed large, hollow thorns in which colonies of a particular species of ant live. The trees also provide food for the ants in the form of special structures on the tips of the leaves. In return the ants protect the acacias from other insects and plants.

If the ants left, the trees would be overrun by vines that would strangle them, and by other insects that would eat their leaves and burrow into the bark. Both ants and trees benefit from this relationship.

Groups or populations of organisms that occupy the same area, and interchange materials and energy among them, make up a community. All organisms need energy to survive. Energy flows through an ecosystem in the form of food. Green plants are the producers that turn the energy of sunlight into energy for growth through a process called photosynthesis. Animals cannot produce their own food so they eat plants and each other. They are called consumers. Decomposers, like fungi and microscopic bacteria, are another important part of the ecosystem. They feed on dead plants and animals, and recycle the materials back into the community.

In nature, each species occupies a different place in its ecosystem, depending on different things for food. This means that each ecosystem can support a great diversity of animals and plants. An organism's place in an ecosystem is called its niche.

## The earth's surface

The surface of the earth is far from smooth. Massive forces within the earth have thrown up mighty mountain chains, such as the Himalayas, and the erosive power of water has worn away the land, even carving deep valleys such as the Grand Canyon.

There are mountains and plateaux, mighty rivers like the Amazon, great plains like the Serengeti, deltas and swamps like the Okavango in Southern Africa, and extraordinary islands like the volcanoes that form the Hawaiian archipelago. This diversity of landforms supports an enormous variety of life forms.

The Hawaiian islands, for example, support an unusual and diverse range of plants and animals. These islands, the most isolated in the world, are formed by a chain of volcanoes that rise from the sea floor. There is a great range of types of landscape on these small islands, from beaches to high mountains to lava deserts but, being so far from other land masses, there are no naturally occurring freshwater fish, amphibians, reptiles or land mammals. This means that other types of animals, such as birds, have occupied the vacant niches. Most plant and animal species that live on the Hawaiian islands occur nowhere else in the world.

*Plants are able to establish themselves in almost any environment – even on recently deposited volcanic lava.*

**Plants**

There are over 300,000 different species of land plants on earth and they have adapted to almost every environment on this planet, from deserts where it hardly ever rains to the cold Antarctic valleys.

Plants have evolved into extraordinary forms to survive in this broad range of environments. The welwitschia plant, which lives in the deserts of Namibia in southern Africa, survives for hundreds of years by gathering droplets of fog on two large, leathery leaves. In the tropical forests of South-east Asia there are plants that depend on flies for pollination and have flowers that look and smell like rotting meat to attract these flies.

A major feature of the earth's surface is the vegetation. Plants make up most of the living matter on this planet. Where different sorts of plants grow depends on the physical factors of light, temperature, the type of soil and the amount of water available. These physical factors vary

*As you go up a mountain the climate becomes cooler and wetter. As a result, the type of vegetation found at various altitudes can be very different. This diagram shows how vegetation changes with altitude in three areas of the world.*

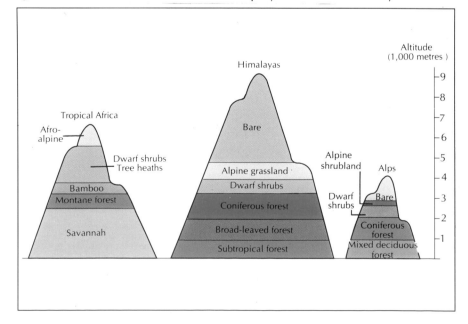

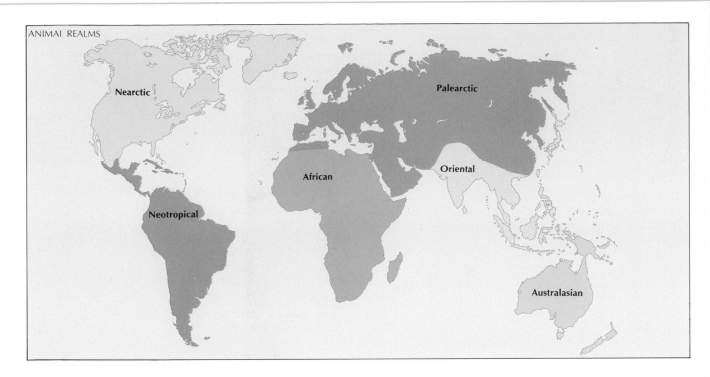

ANIMAL REALMS

Nearctic

Palearctic

African

Oriental

Neotropical

Australasian

*Zoologists have divided the world into six realms, based on the similarities between the animals that live in each region.*

according to the climate, and the climate varies according to the latitude – where a place lies between the North or South Pole and the Equator. Near the Equator it is hot and wet while near the poles it is very cold; in between lie the temperate regions and the deserts.

Climate also changes according to altitude. In biological terms, climbing a mountain is like making a much longer journey towards the poles – the higher you go the cooler and wetter it usually becomes.

As the climate changes, the vegetation changes. Even in the tropics there are mountains, such as Mt. Kilimanjaro in Tanzania, that have plants which are quite like those in the Arctic. The climatic variations with latitude and altitude mean that vegetation can be classified into broad zones which scientists call biomes. Communities of plants under similar climatic conditions develop along similar lines and different species often adopt similar forms. The world's principal biomes are shown on the map on pages 6 and 7.

### Animals

Animals inhabit almost every part of the earth's surface. Though the tiger in India is very different from the possum in Australia,

and the sloth of South America is very different from the hedgehog of Europe, there are surprising similarities between the groups of animals that inhabit the different continents. In Europe, for example, there are snakes and frogs, butterflies and spiders, earthworms and snails. In Australia, on the other side of the world, you will find the same sorts of animals. They will not be exactly alike but they are clearly from the same family.

*There are animals living on almost every part of the earth's surface. This bighorn sheep has found itself a precarious perch.*

These animals have common ancestors; yet how did they come to be so far apart? Scientists have discovered that continents move very slowly and by only a few centimetres a year. This movement has been going on for hundreds of millions of years, and is caused by the same massive forces within the earth that push up mountain chains. Originally all the continents were joined together into one supercontinent called Pangaea, on which early forms of animals, like primitive snakes and frogs, evolved. At various times, some continents split off and began to drift away, carrying with them collections of animals.

The different times at which continents broke away from each other and the length of time they have been isolated explains the differences between the animals on different continents. Australia separated from Pangaea very early and so many of its animals are unique. The marsupials, such as the kangaroo, which carry their young in a pouch, occur almost nowhere else in the world. Scientists have divided the world of animals up into six principal realms, which are shown on the map on page 11.

As continents and islands drifted apart they became isolated from each other, and the animals which inhabited them evolved in different ways. One example is the island of Madagascar which drifted away from the African continent tens of millions of years ago. Originally it would have had the same groups of animals that then existed in Africa, but they have since evolved into a unique and unusual collection of species. For example elsewhere in Africa, lemurs have been displaced by monkeys and have died out, but there are twenty-five species of lemur on Madagascar, some of which have only recently been discovered. Half of the world's species of chameleons – small lizards that can change the colour of their skin to match that of their surroundings – live on Madagascar.

**Above** *Lemurs live only on the island of Madagascar.*

**Left** *A deep-sea angler fish waits to attract prey with its glowing lure.*

WORLD MAP OF SEA-BED

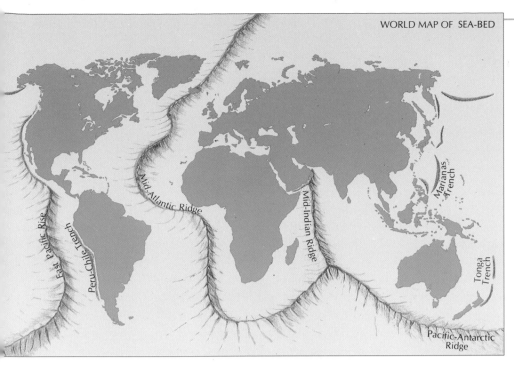

Mid-Atlantic Ridge

Mid-Indian Ridge

East Pacific Rise

Peru-Chile Trench

Marianas Trench

Tonga Trench

Pacific-Antarctic Ridge

**Left** *It was once thought that the sea-bed was a flat, featureless plain, but scientists have found that there are mountain ranges, deep trenches, cliffs and plateaux.*

**Below** *Emperor penguins on the ice of Antarctica – the world's last great wilderness.*

## The sea

Over 70 per cent of our planet's surface is covered by oceans and seas. Earth is the only planet that has large areas covered by water; the others are too hot or too cold and any water that existed has either frozen or evaporated. It is water that makes life possible on earth and the oceans are home to a huge number of plants and animal species.

Life in the sea is divided into zones that are based on depth. There is the tidal zone, where the sea meets the land. Then there are the shallow continental shelves that surround the land masses. Most life in the sea lives in these two shallowest zones as there is plentiful light available for photosynthesis. Beyond the continental shelf in the ocean basins there are two more zones, one of light and another of perpetual darkness. Light does not pass very well through water and the deeper you go the darker it gets. Below about 200 metres light does not penetrate at all and it is always dark.

Extraordinary life forms inhabit the ocean depths. Giant squid live at 450 metres, and sometimes sperm whales will dive down to these depths to eat the squid. As there is no light in the depths there are no plants that produce food by means of photosynthesis. Therefore, the organisms that live here must depend for food on debris that falls from above, or prey on each other. The angler fish has a permanent lure that projects from its forehead, almost like a fishing rod. It has a lighted tip that hangs in front of its mouth. Small fish are attracted to this glowing tip in the dark of the ocean depths and are eaten by the angler fish.

## Wilderness

Wilderness is the natural world in its original, unaltered state. It is the part of the earth's surface that is uncultivated or uninhabited by humans. In fact, in many places that are considered to be wilderness there are people living, whether it is the Yanomamo Indians in the Amazon rainforest or sheep farmers on Dartmoor in south-west England. Wilderness is very important as it preserves the diversity of nature as a living, functioning whole.

There are few places left that are wilderness in the sense of being uninhabited. Antarctica is, perhaps, the last great wilderness, and even this frozen continent is threatened with human interference.

# THE HUMAN WORLD

If you could view the earth from deep space, you would not see the effect of people on the planet. But in this century, people have had more effect on the global environment than they have done in the previous millions of years of human history.

Part of the reason is the large increase in the number of people on earth. Today, there are over 5.2 billion people – that is 5.2 thousand million individual persons or lives. Each day, another quarter of a million people are added to the population.

This population has grown rapidly over the last 200 years, and although growth rates are now slowing down, they may not even out for another 100 years or so.

The world map below shows how quickly the populations of the countries of the world are growing. Although the percentage increase figures may seem small, the populations of certain countries grow quickly. For example, a 4 per cent

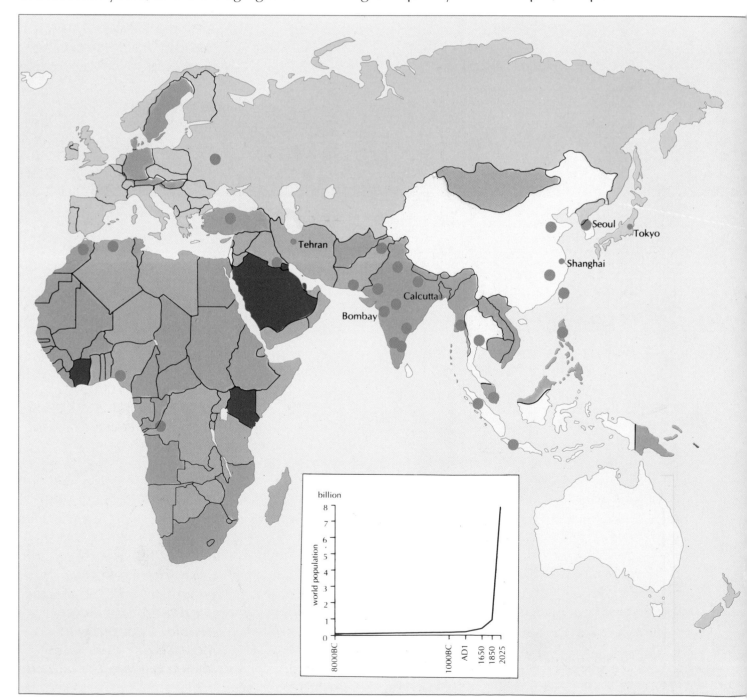

billion

world population

8000BC   1000BC  AD1  1650  1850  2025

increase each year means that a country's population will double in just over 17 years.

**People on earth**

For many thousands of years, the number of people on earth has increased only very gradually. The graph on page 14 shows how the level of population kept fairly even until about the year 1600, since when the rate of increase has quickened.

The estimated world population in 8000 BC was only about 5 million people – around two-thirds the size of London's population today. By AD 1, it was about 150 million and by 1650, it had reached 500 million. It then took 200 years to double to 1,000 million (1 billion), and only about 80 years to double again to 2 billion by the 1930s. By 1975, just 45 years later, it had reached 4 billion, and is expected to top 8 billion by the year 2025.

**Above** *An old people's home in Germany. In developed countries people live longer than in developing countries, because they are wealthier and health care is better.*

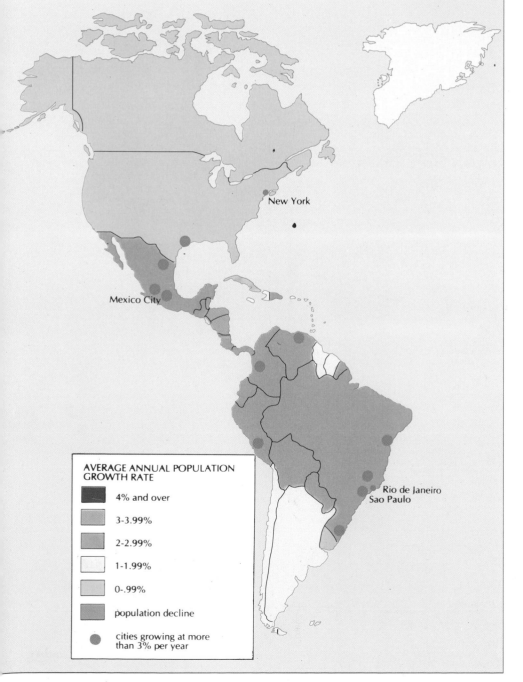

New York

Mexico City

Rio de Janeiro
Sao Paulo

AVERAGE ANNUAL POPULATION GROWTH RATE

- 4% and over
- 3-3.99%
- 2-2.99%
- 1-1.99%
- 0-.99%
- population decline
- cities growing at more than 3% per year

*This map shows how fast the population is increasing in different countries, and highlights the fastest-growing cities. The cities named on the map will be the world's largest in the year 2000.*

*These growth-rate figures do not tell the whole story; China has a relatively low growth-rate but, because it has a huge number of people, its population increased by over 13.6 million between 1985 and 1990.*

The rapid rise in world population began in the first countries to industrialize – those in Western Europe especially. The growth or decline in any population depends on the birth-rate and the death-rate. If, each year, around the same number of people are born and die, the total population stays at the same level. But, from the seventeenth century, people began to live longer as health and food supplies improved. Eventually, in developed countries, increasing prosperity led to a lowering of the birth-rate. Today the population in the developed countries is growing very slowly or declining.

About 90 per cent of the increase in world population is now in the developing countries. Since the 1940s the death-rate has fallen in most developing countries, mostly through control of disease. At the same time, the birth-rate has risen. Taken together, these two trends have resulted in rapidly increasing populations in most countries in the developing world.

For parent couples in the developing world, there are good reasons for having many children. Most people are very poor by Western standards, and there are normally very few health and social services provided, particularly in rural areas. So children are seen as an investment – they are able to work and bring in income to the family and provide help and security for parents in their old age. But some children die young, so more children need to be born to help the family. Over 14 million children die before the age of 5, and most of these are in the developing world.

Although birth-rates are beginning to fall in many developing countries, they are still high. World population may not stop rising until the year 2100, by which time it may have reached 14 billion. This would put great strain on the resources and life-support systems of the planet, such as the soil, water and atmosphere. It may be possible to prevent the population from reaching such a high figure, but that depends on action taken today.

The most effective way of tackling high birth-rates is to improve people's lives. Making birth-control more widely available is part of the solution, but tackling poverty, providing better health care and education,

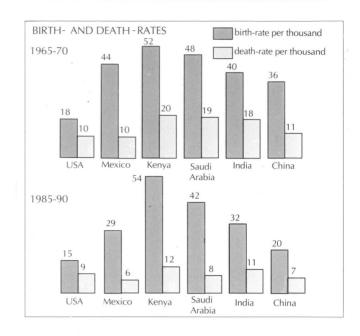

*A country's population grows when the birth-rate is higher than the death-rate.*

and raising the status of women in developing countries are more effective in reducing the number of children born.

**The city people**
More and more people are living in cities. At the beginning of this century only around 10 per cent of the world's population lived in cities but, by the year 2000, nearly half will live in an urban area.

As with population growth, the increase in the size of cities began in the industrialized countries first. The Industrial Revolution of the eighteenth and nineteenth centuries led to the growth of major cities in the Western countries. By 1960, six out of the ten largest cities in the world were located in these industrialized countries. But by the year 2000, only two such cities – Tokyo and New York – will be in this top ten list; the other eight will be in developing nations.

The giant cities of the developing world are growing much faster than the cities in the developed world have ever done. One reason for this is population increase; the other reason is the migration of people from rural areas to towns and cities.

**Right** *The proportion of the population living in cities is growing in many parts of the world, but especially in developing countries. By the year 2000, most of the world's largest cities will be in developing nations.*

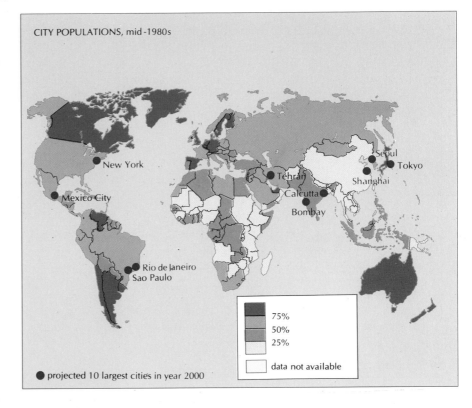

CITY POPULATIONS, mid-1980s

New York
Mexico City
Rio de Janeiro
Sao Paulo
Tehran
Calcutta
Bombay
Seoul
Tokyo
Shanghai

75%
50%
25%
data not available

● projected 10 largest cities in year 2000

**Below** *This village in Burkina Faso is now deserted. Its people have moved away in the hope of finding a better life in the city.*

Two different forces combine to cause people to migrate to cities. Forces which 'push' people from the land and others which 'pull' them towards the cities. Some of the push factors are: the difficulty of making a living in rural areas; poor land; lack of wood for fuel; loss of land which has been taken for growing crops for export; and increasing mechanization. In some areas famine or war may be other important reasons for migration.

The pull factors which attract people to the cities include the chance of a job, help from relatives in the city, cheaper food, and more chance of health care and education.

Migration is resulting in the growth of large shanty towns or slums around most of the big cities in the developing world. Some of these squatter settlements are so large they form areas the size of cities themselves. Because the people are poor, they have to squat on the poorest land, which is unfit for housing. It may suffer

from flooding, be situated on a hillside, or next to polluting industry or the city dump. Often there are no services – water, electricity, refuse collection or sewers – but people have nowhere else to go. Often they are resourceful and can improve their settlements over time, but the pressure of new arrivals makes lasting improvement difficult.

The rapid growth of cities in developing countries puts pressure on the environment, particularly through air and water pollution. Poor urban dwellers are often the first to suffer the effects of this pollution. To tackle these problems, city and national governments need to help the squatter settlements by providing basic services. They also have to reduce migration to the cities by tackling poverty in the rural areas.

*This shanty town outside Manila, the capital of the Philippines, is built on top of a rubbish tip.*

Many cities in developed countries are also facing problems. Air pollution, noise, and traffic congestion are problems that all large cities have to deal with. But unlike the cities in the developing world, those in the developed world can afford more easily to tackle their problems.

### Rich world, poor world
Many people point to the world's growing population as the reason for our environmental problems. However, although population size is important, the way in which resources are used by different groups of people is also crucial.

The environment is being damaged by

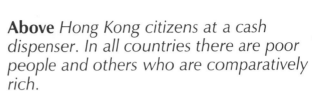

**Above** *Hong Kong citizens at a cash dispenser. In all countries there are poor people and others who are comparatively rich.*

extremes of wealth and poverty within countries, but more particularly between countries. Less than a quarter of the world's population (about 1.2 billion people) live in the developed nations but they consume three-quarters of the world's resources and enjoy two-thirds of the world's income. This unequal sharing of resources is

**Below** *This map shows the wealth of countries, in terms of each country's gross national product per capita – the total value of the goods and services it produces in a year divided by its population.*

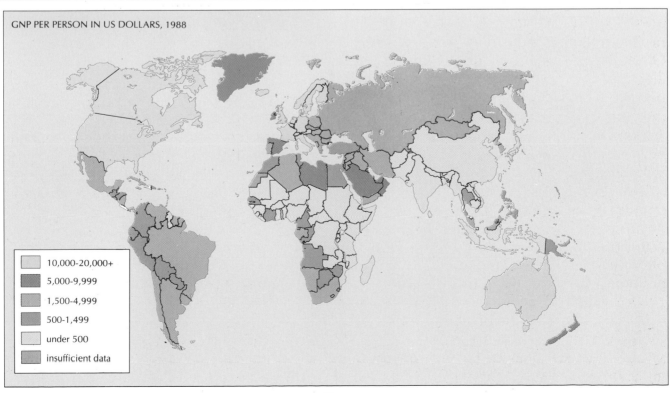

GNP PER PERSON IN US DOLLARS, 1988

- 10,000-20,000+
- 5,000-9,999
- 1,500-4,999
- 500-1,499
- under 500
- insufficient data

perpetuated by the richer nations who depend on the raw materials produced in developing countries – such as metal ores, textiles and food materials – to maintain their wealthy, industrialized economies.

Unfortunately, the developing nations do not get a fair price for their goods or commodities. The richer countries are able to control the market prices, and in the 1980s many of the commodity prices dropped. Meanwhile, the prices of manufactured goods and oil that the developing countries need to buy have gone up. This means the terms of trade are in the developed countries' favour.

This problem is made worse by the debt crisis. In the 1970s many developing countries borrowed money from the developed countries and Western banks to finance development projects, such as dams and industrial plants. They had to pay interest on the loans, but soon interest rates went up steeply. By the 1980s many countries were having difficulty in paying the interest.

Some countries such as Brazil, Mexico and Argentina have increased the area of land devoted to 'cash crops' for export, to try and earn more money. This leaves less land available for the rural poor, who have in turn been forced to overgraze their land, resulting in soil erosion and migration to the cities. At the same time, the debt crisis has meant that developing countries have had little money available for providing basic services such as clean water, housing, health and education – which would help reduce the birth-rate. They have also had few funds for protecting the environment.

In global terms, the debt crisis and unequal trade terms mean that the poorer countries lose more to the richer countries than they gain from them. The developing nations pay over US$50 billion a year more than they receive in new loans or aid from the developed countries. Over the last few decades, the rich countries have been getting richer while the poor have become poorer.

This situation also applies to the sharing of wealth within countries. In the developed world increasing numbers of people are living on income support, – money provided by governments to help those on low incomes. But in most cities in developing countries the extremes of poverty and wealth are greater and more visible. About a quarter of the world's

*This plantation in the Philippines grows pineapples as a cash crop. The fruit is exported to richer countries.*

population now lives in deep poverty.

The earth's resources are limited. This means that they have to be shared much more equally and used much more carefully. Resources need to be used carefully if future generations are to be able to meet their needs. The idea of sustainable development, which tries to develop economic activity that does not harm the local or global ecological balance, is beginning to catch on. It involves the

*These children in Jakarta, the capital of Indonesia, are scavenging among rubbish for anything that they might be able to sell.*

efficient use of energy and resources, recycling, and keeping waste to a minimum. In developing countries in particular, it means creating projects that are based on people's real needs, and which protect rather than destroy the local culture and ecology.

# FALLING FORESTS

Forests are much more than collections of trees. They are the natural vegetation of over 40 per cent of the earth's land surface and include some of the most complex ecosystems on the planet. There are many different types of forest. Each is made up of different kinds of trees and has a whole range of plant and animal life adapted to living within it. Although the same general type of forest can be found in different continents, each contains its own unique species. So if a forest in one part of the world is damaged or destroyed, many forms of life may disappear from the face of the earth.

*The world's forest and woodland areas. Where a particular type of forest grows depends upon the climate and the kind of soil that is present. The inset picture shows the trees that are found most commonly in certain types of forest.*

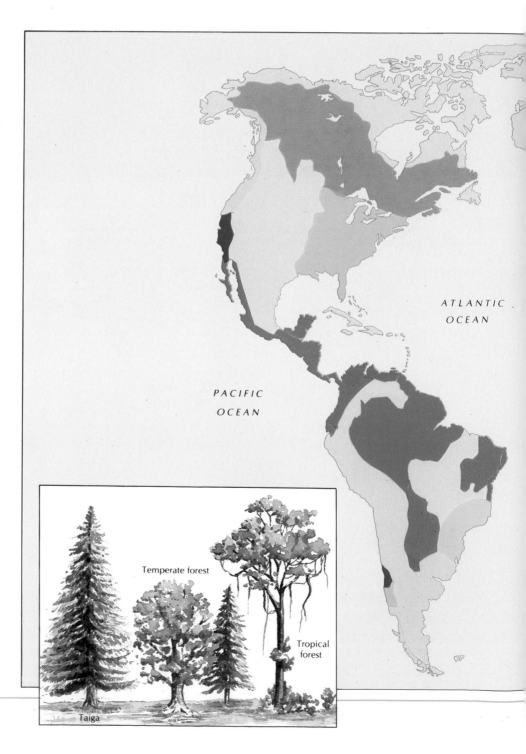

ATLANTIC
OCEAN

PACIFIC
OCEAN

Temperate forest

Tropical
forest

Taiga

### Life in the rainforest

Tropical rainforests are made up of several layers. Each layer has its own world of plants and animals which all depend on each other. The trees depend on animals to pollinate them and spread their seeds, and the animals depend on trees for their food and shelter.

The highest layer in a rainforest is the canopy, over 30 metres above the ground, formed by the crowns of tall trees. The canopy has more life than any other part of the forest as it receives most of the rain and sunlight. The trees flower and produce fruit all year round providing food for birds, insects, bats and monkeys. Other animals, including some squirrels, lizards, frogs and even snakes, are specially adapted to spend their whole lives in the treetops.

Up to 15 metres above the ground smaller trees, such as palms or young saplings, form another layer – the understorey. Here it is quiet and humid. The leaves provide food for a few large mammals, like deer, okapi and tapirs. These animals are hunted by carnivores.

On the forest floor the light is very dim. Only a few plants which can survive in the shade live there. Fallen leaves, dead branches and even tree trunks decay very rapidly in these hot, damp surroundings due to multitudes of fungi, insects and other organisms which feed on decomposing matter. The minerals produced by decaying trees are taken up again by the living trees' shallow roots, so much of the material is quickly recycled before it can be washed away by rain.

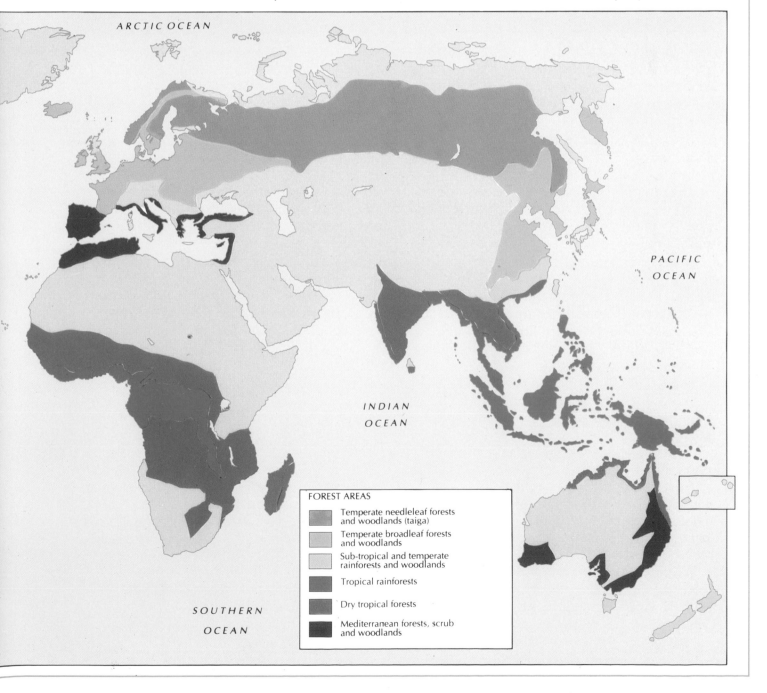

ARCTIC OCEAN

PACIFIC OCEAN

INDIAN OCEAN

SOUTHERN OCEAN

FOREST AREAS

Temperate needleleaf forests and woodlands (taiga)

Temperate broadleaf forests and woodlands

Sub-tropical and temperate rainforests and woodlands

Tropical rainforests

Dry tropical forests

Mediterranean forests, scrub and woodlands

### Different kinds of forest

The forests of Northern Canada and the USSR are known as **taiga**. They have evergreen coniferous trees like pines, spruces and firs. Here the winters are long and intensely cold, rainfall is low and the soils are poor and sandy. These conifers provide 'softwood' which is made into paper for printing, packaging and babies' nappies; and plywood and wood for building houses and making pine furniture.

In the middle latitudes, where the temperature is above 10°C for at least half the year and the annual rainfall is over 40 cm, **broad-leaved deciduous forests** are the natural vegetation. In Europe these forests contain oaks, beeches, birches, limes, chestnuts and elms. In the USA maples and hickories are also common woodland trees. Much of these forests have been cleared over the last 2,000 years to make room for farming and places for people to live.

Further south, particularly on eastern continental coasts where there is less danger of frost, there are broad-leaved evergreen forests, also known as **temperate rainforest**. They are made up of trees called southern beeches, and conifers like the Kauri Pine or the Chile Pine.

**Tropical rainforests** are found in countries all along the Equator, but mainly in three great blocks – Amazonia, the Congo and South-east Asia. Here the temperature and

*An aerial view of mangrove trees and Nipa palms in Brunei, South-east Asia. Mangroves grow in tropical climates, usually along river banks.*

rainfall are high all year round. Thousands of different types of plant grow in tropical rainforests, including creepers, climbers and ferns, but the most important are the huge evergreen trees that form the forest canopy. Tropical rainforests are vanishing fast due to logging, burning and mining by developers, settlers and farmers.

Where there is an annual dry season, **dry tropical forest** may form the natural vegetation. There are several different types, including the monsoon forests of India and Myanmar where teak is important, and the savannah woodland of Africa where acacia trees are common. These forests are in even greater danger than rainforests as people clear the land for cattle grazing or cut the trees for firewood.

Where the summers are hot and dry, and the winters warm and wet, what is known as **Mediterranean forest** – another kind of evergreen forest – grows, made up of evergreen oaks and other plants with small, tough leaves which can withstand drought. Eucalyptus forests in Australia are similar. Much of this forest has been destroyed by forest fires and the development of tourist resorts along the coasts.

The removal of just one forest tree, even by natural causes, affects all the plants around it. Some of the shade-loving plants in lower layers may die in the fierce light and heat of the sun. Other seedlings, unable to grow in the shade, now shoot up and eventually close the gap in the canopy. Where trees are felled the forest cannot easily grow back. When a tree is cut down, as many as twenty others may be seriously damaged as it falls or by the machinery used to take it away. Once a large patch of the forest floor is laid bare the heavy tropical rains wash away the minerals, seeds and even the soil.

The wealth of plant life in rainforests has misled people to think these areas would be ideal for farmland. In fact the soil is usually very poor. After two or three seasons of growing crops like maize or coffee the land is so infertile that only sparse, coarse grass can grow.

## Why forests are important to people

Trees provided shelter, firewood, tools and food for the first humans. As society developed, some forests were cleared to grow crops. Wood was cut from forests for buildings and tools or to make charcoal for smelting metals. The remaining forest was left as hunting grounds and as places where people could collect fruits, nuts, fungi, honey and other forest products for food and medicines.

Forests have also been linked to magic or religious beliefs. Even today, people regard forests – or their remnants, woods – with a sense of wonder and pleasure. Many millions of people all over the world still depend on forests for their living – through tourism as well as logging, hunting and gathering.

*Lush vegetation in the rainforest of Costa Rica, Central America.*

Forests are also important to people in less obvious ways. They help to keep the balance of nature in the air, water and soil. Trees and other plants use the energy in sunlight to take carbon dioxide from the air. They convert it to sugars and other substances which make up the body of the plant. In this process, which is called photosynthesis, they give out oxygen. Like all other living things plants respire to release energy to grow. As a result, carbon dioxide goes back into the atmosphere. The carbon trapped in plants is also released as carbon dioxide when plants are burnt or when they die.

Some scientists fear that the rapid destruction of forests, particularly the burning of tropical forests, is adding to the 'greenhouse effect'. The large amounts of carbon dioxide produced by burning trees go into the atmosphere, adding to the layer of gases that are already there. These gases act like the glass roof of a greenhouse – allowing sunlight to enter and trapping some of the sun's heat. If some heat were not trapped by the atmosphere, the earth would be far too cold for living things to exist; but if there are too many greenhouse gases, too much heat will be trapped.

There is growing concern this could cause global warming which might have a dramatic effect on the world climate, but there is no clear evidence yet.

There is, however, evidence to show that forests affect local climates

This area of rainforest in Brazil is being cleared so that the land can be used for agriculture. The soil is not very fertile, and will have to be abandoned within 2 or 3 years.

or the weather. Trees, like other plants, take up water through their roots and lose it through their leaves. That is why the air in and around forests is always moist. In hot tropical regions such large amounts of water are lost from the trees that

clouds form above the forest. Much of the rain that falls is then absorbed again by tree roots.

Trees also prevent soil erosion. Their roots bind the soil together and help to prevent it being washed away. Their leaves and branches bear the force of heavy rains and protect the soil surface as the water can only trickle or drip down. In this way forests act as giant sponges, soaking up water and allowing any excess to flow gently downhill.

tropical rainforests.

European forests are fairly young. Until the end of the last ice age, about 10,000 years ago, huge areas of the earth, including much of Europe, were covered with ice and snow.

A hectare of British woodland has mostly oak or beech trees with fewer than 20 other kinds of tree or shrub. In an area of tropical rainforest the same size you could find 200 different sorts of trees. Each type of tree has many hundreds of animals – mammals, reptiles, birds and insects – living on or close to it.

**Above** *Deforestation caused this landslide in Malaysia. In the background a truck carries away more felled trees.*

In northern regions, including parts of Canada and the European Alps, evergreen forests on mountainsides help protect the villages below from avalanches. In tropical climates, where the rainfall is often sudden and very heavy, forest-covered slopes prevent flooding and mud-slides which could cause death and damage to millions of people living in the valleys. Forests on hills and mountainsides also stop the soils of fertile farmland being slowly washed away.

### Forests as wildlife reservoirs

Forests are important as home to millions of species of plants and animals. The forests that are richest in plant and animal life are found at the Equator, where the climate has stayed the same for millions of years. The first flowering plants may have evolved in these

**Below** *Forests are home to many species of plants and animals.*

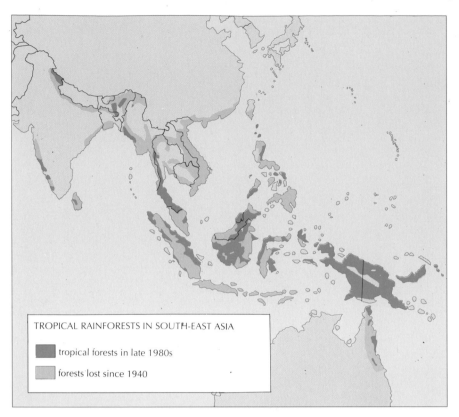

**Left** *The vanishing rainforests of South-east Asia. By the year 2000, Thailand will have lost 60 per cent of the tropical forest it had in 1981.*

**Right** *Logs are floated downstream to a wood-pulp mill in Quebec province, Canada.*

**Below** *The construction of a new road cuts a deep scar through the Amazon rainforest.*

TROPICAL RAINFORESTS IN SOUTH-EAST ASIA

tropical forests in late 1980s

forests lost since 1940

Conservationists are concerned about the destruction of all forests, but especially tropical rainforests, because so many types of plants and animals live there. Only 7 per cent of the earth's surface is covered by tropical forests, yet they contain more than half the species found on this planet. Most of these will vanish with the forests, before we have had a chance to find out anything about them.

Some plants from tropical forests are useful for medicines, for the local people and for us. For example, quinine – a drug used to treat malaria – comes from the bark of a tropical tree. The rosy periwinkle from the forests of Madagascar is used to make a drug that combats a form of cancer in children.

Other forest plants are relatives of crops that we use for food, such as bananas, oranges and coffee. The wild plants are needed to help us grow new varieties that produce more food and are resistant to diseases.

### The vanishing forests

Scientists cannot agree on how fast or how seriously people are damaging and destroying forests. However, they do agree that forests are vanishing rapidly and, year by year, the forest that remains is disappearing even faster.

As much as 20 million hectares of tropical forest may be destroyed or damaged each year. This is an area the size of six football pitches every minute. About half the world's tropical rainforests have disappeared in the last 50 years, and at the present rate much of what is left could be damaged beyond repair by the year 2000.

In the past, logging methods were not so destructive to forests as they are today. It took two men more than a day to fell a tropical hardwood tree with axes and handsaws. Elephants or buffalo then pulled the timber to logging camps and the logs were floated down rivers. Nowadays one man can fell many trees in a day using a chain saw. Heavy machines, like giant tractors, drag the trunks to depots where trucks take them to towns and ports.

There are many reasons why forests are destroyed, but the most important is money. Governments in tropical countries allow logging companies to cut down trees as a quick way of obtaining money for their countries. They need to pay for schools, hospitals, clean water and housing for their growing populations, or to pay back money borrowed from wealthier countries. Over one-third of the tropical timber felled comes to Europe, which is the second most important timber market in the world after Japan. Raw wood and chipboard, which were once huge tropical trees, are made into furniture, doors and even toilet seats!

Roads made by logging companies open up the forests to settlers. In many countries, especially in Latin America and South-east Asia, most of the best farmland is owned by a few rich people, and millions of poor people have no land at all. Poor families often move to forest areas and clear the land to grow food. Sometimes the government encourages them to do this instead of moving to overcrowded cities.

Tropical forests are often cut down to make plantations of so-called 'cash crops' such as tea, coffee, tobacco, sugar, cotton and palm oil. The plantations provide work for thousands of people and the country gets money by exporting the cash crops to rich countries overseas. In Central and South America forests have been burnt to make grassland for cattle; much of the meat produced is sold abroad.

Some governments, international banks and overseas aid agencies, like the World Bank, have lent money to developing countries for projects which destroy rainforests. These include building hydro-electric dams, mining, cash crop farming, plantations and cattle ranching. Many of these projects fail, but the country still has to repay the loan.

About 2 billion people use wood to cook food, boil water and keep themselves warm. Rapid population growth and increasing poverty mean people are cutting down trees faster than they can be replaced. This is one of the main threats to the drier tropical forests of Africa and Asia.

It is not only tropical forests that are endangered, however. In temperate regions trees are also under threat. Around 2,000 years ago, most of Northern Europe was covered with forests. Today what little forest remains is mostly in national parks or protected areas. The rest has been cleared to grow crops, graze animals, provide places for people to live and work or to mine the minerals in the earth below. Even what is left of the temperate forests is not safe. Millions of hectares of trees throughout Europe may be suffering from the effects of acid rain (see Chapter 7).

**Above** *Trees killed by acid rain in Germany's Black Forest.*

**Paying the price**
• In Thailand, more than 350 people were killed in November 1988 when villages were washed away by floods. The forests on the hills had been cut down for timber and to make fields to grow crops.
• In Sarawak, Malaysia, many Penans – one of the last forest people in the world – have been arrested for blockading logging roads. They are protesting that timber companies are destroying their way of life. Fishing, game, sago, rattan and other forests products have all become scarce since the loggers opened up the area.
• In 1983 a fire in Kalimantan, Indonesia, destroyed an area of swamp forest bigger than Belgium. Two years later the peaty soil was still smouldering. It is not known how the fire started, but dead wood left behind by loggers helped it spread out of control.
• Nine iron smelters and two cement factories are planned in the Amazon forest of Brazil. Funds for the Grande Carajas Programme have come mainly from the European Community (EC). At least 1.5 million hectares of forest will be cut down to make charcoal for these industries. The survival of 27 tribes of Indians who live there is threatened.
• The lakes which supply water to the Panama Canal in Central America are slowly filling up with soil washed down from the surrounding hills. The forests there have been cleared by poor farmers who have moved up to the hillsides because richer farmers have taken the better land. If this continues there will not be enough water for large ships to pass through the locks in the canal.
• Severe flooding in Bangladesh affected 85 per cent of the country in 1988. In the past, when the lower Himalayas were covered with trees, flood disasters only happened twice a century. By the 1970s terrible floods were happening every 4 years.

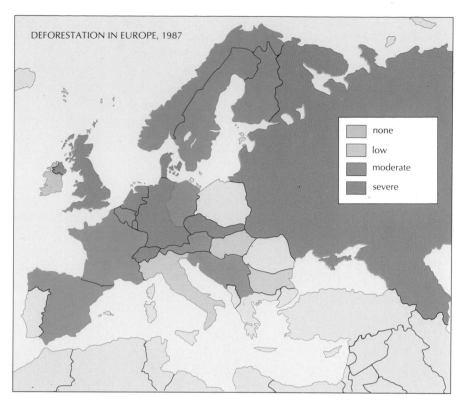

DEFORESTATION IN EUROPE, 1987

| | |
|---|---|
| | none |
| | low |
| | moderate |
| | severe |

**Below** *Deforested land being used for cattle ranching in Brazil. Some of the beef produced will be sold abroad to be made into hamburgers.*

**Above** *Deforestation does not affect tropical rainforests alone. As this map shows, the temperate forests of Europe are also being destroyed.*

Organizations like the World Wide Fund for Nature and Friends of the Earth can put pressure on governments to protect forests by setting up national parks and nature reserves. They also raise money to look after these forests and do scientific research.

However, we cannot protect all the world's remaining forests like this. The best way is to encourage people to use only small parts of the forests to make money without cutting them down. Some temperate forests can be used carefully to provide timber. Tropical forests produce far more than just wood – nuts, oils, spices, dyes, fish and game can all be harvested without harming the forests. Forest people have been doing this for thousands of years.

We can all help by trying to use wood from plantations or specially managed projects where trees are replanted to replace those that have been cut down. If people in rich countries were to stop buying timber and furniture from tropical rainforests, logging would decrease.

## Saving the forests

There are many reasons why forests are being damaged and destroyed in the world, and no easy solutions to the problem. Everyone has to share the responsibility – governments, organizations and individuals.

# FOOD AND FARMING

Today 5.2 billion people must share the food resources of the globe. By the year 2000 there will be an extra billion mouths to feed and experts estimate we will need 40 per cent more food than we already grow. During the last 50 years, intensive farming methods – using machines, fertilizers and pesticides – have been used to increase crop yields. However, these methods carry a huge environmental cost. In many areas over-use of farmland has destroyed the fertility of the soil, chemicals have polluted the land and waste from livestock farming has poisoned the water. Wildlife habitats have also been destroyed in the quest to increase the amount of land under cultivation. If these problems are to be avoided in the future, we will have to find new ways of growing food that will put back into the earth as much as we take out, if not more. Otherwise hunger and famine will only increase.

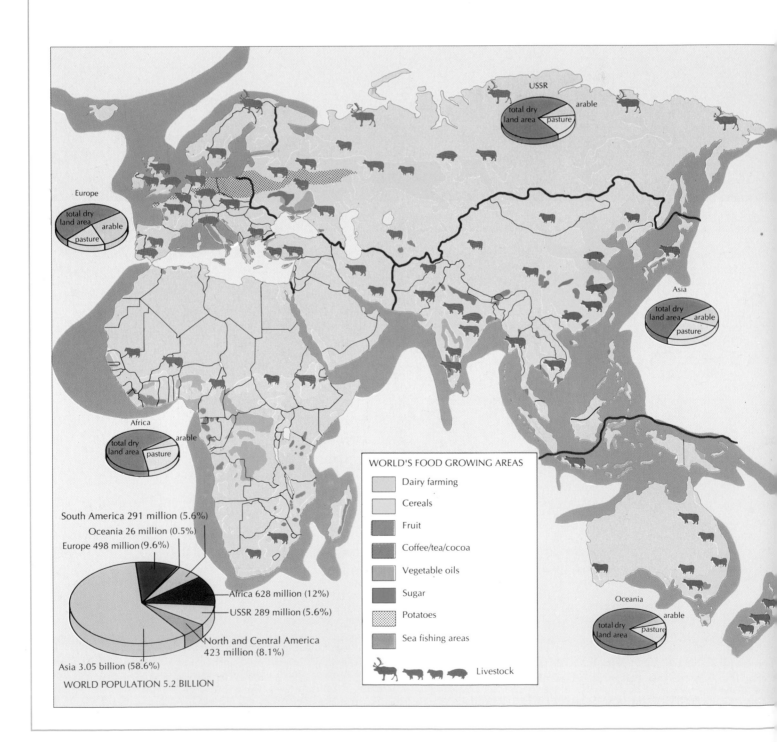

USSR
total dry land area — arable — pasture

Europe
total dry land area — arable — pasture

Asia
total dry land area — arable — pasture

Africa
total dry land area — arable — pasture

Oceania
total dry land area — arable — pasture

WORLD'S FOOD GROWING AREAS
- Dairy farming
- Cereals
- Fruit
- Coffee/tea/cocoa
- Vegetable oils
- Sugar
- Potatoes
- Sea fishing areas
- Livestock

South America 291 million (5.6%)
Oceania 26 million (0.5%)
Europe 498 million (9.6%)
Africa 628 million (12%)
USSR 289 million (5.6%)
North and Central America 423 million (8.1%)
Asia 3.05 billion (58.6%)

WORLD POPULATION 5.2 BILLION

### How agriculture began

Early humans fed themselves by hunting wild animals and gathering plants, nuts and fruits. Agriculture, or the cultivation of soil, first developed around 10,000 years ago when people started to grow food crops on the fertile floodplains and deltas of various rivers, such as the Nile in Egypt, the Yangtze in China, and the Tigris and Euphrates in Mesopotamia.

These first farmers selected wild plants and developed ways to grow and harvest them as foodstuffs. Later, in steep and hilly areas, farmers built level terraces on the slopes to make the land easier to cultivate. In drier areas they constructed dams and channels to capture precious water and deliver it to the fields. In some places people have practised shifting cultivation for centuries, moving on every few years to clear a new plot of land.

### Land use and soil fertility

Today we cultivate 11 per cent of the total dry area of the globe. Some experts say we could double this, but others doubt that many of the unused areas are fertile enough to grow crops.

The distribution of soil fertility is very uneven. For instance, in Europe fertile soils cover more than 36 per cent of the land area and we cultivate more than 80 per cent of these good soils. In hot, wet, tropical regions soil fertility is far more fragile because torrential rain washes away most of the nutrients. In the rainforest a

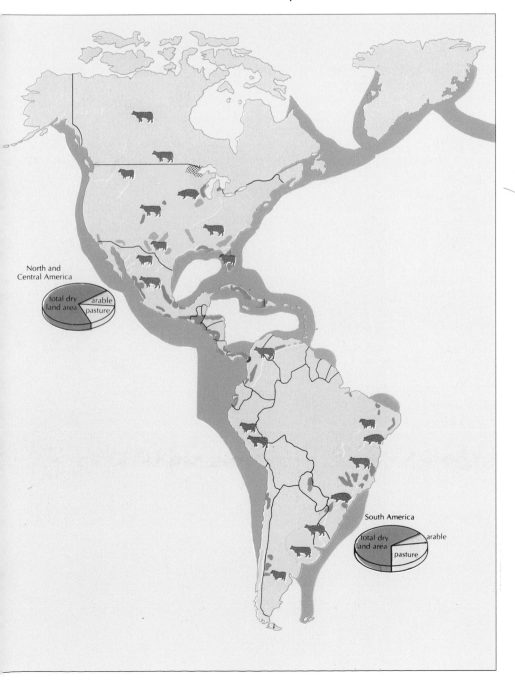

North and Central America

total dry land area — arable — pasture

South America

total dry land area — arable — pasture

*This map shows the main crops grown in each region, together with the most important type of livestock that is raised there – reindeer, cattle, sheep or pigs.*

*The large pie chart shows the population of the world's regions. The small pie charts show how much of the total dry land in each region is used for crop-growing and how much is pasture land. Overall, only 11 per cent of the world's dry land area is used for cultivation.*

small patch of land cleared for planting can be used only for around 3 years, by which time the fertility of the soil will be exhausted. After that the forest must be left to grow back over the land and revive the soil. All over the world, farmers know that they must either allow nature to replenish the soil or add some kind of fertilizer to replace the nutrients they remove through crop cultivation.

## Crops for food

Throughout history people have used as many as 3,000 plant species for food, although only around 150 have been grown commercially – to produce food to be sold. The need to grow more food for bigger populations has led farmers to concentrate on fewer and fewer species, and today most people in the world are fed on less than 20 major crops. Four of these – wheat, rice, potatoes and maize – now account for more than all other food crops combined.

Some regions, such as Latin America, just manage to grow as much food as they need. Others are unable to grow enough. For example, Africa has to feed 11 per cent of the world's population on less than 7 per cent of the planet's total crop production.

The combination of crops such as cassava and sorghum, which have little nutritional value, and regular periods of drought help to make Africa the hungriest region in the world.

North America, Japan, Australia and Western Europe all produce far more food

*Some countries, including many of those in Western Europe, produce more food than they need. These French apples have been left to rot.*

in some Asian countries there is not enough to go round.

Overall, far less food is grown per head of population in the developing countries than in the developed countries, where more food is grown on less land mainly by using artificial fertilizers and pesticides. Developed countries now use on average twice as much fertilizer as developing nations, who frequently cannot afford to import them.

## Livestock farming

At the same time that people began to cultivate crops they also domesticated the wild ancestors of today's grazing animals and poultry. In some places keeping livestock for meat and milk became vital, especially in dry and semi-desert areas where animals eat plants that humans cannot use. Livestock also provide fibres for clothing such as wool, camel hair and leather, and lamp oil. Dung is also a very useful source of fertilizer or fuel.

Meat consumption varies widely around the world. Although the developing countries may possess more than 50 per cent of the world's livestock, they consume less than 20 per cent of the world's meat and milk. Meat consumption in developed countries costs the developing world in other ways: while children die of hunger in Africa at least 40 per cent of the world's edible grain supply is fed to livestock in Europe, the USSR and North America.

than they need. Yet they all import a great deal of food to provide a more varied, though not necessarily healthier, diet. In general they feed their surplus grain production to livestock.

Asia has high rates of food production but there is also a huge population to be fed, so

Other human foods, such as soya beans, are also used in animal feeds.

The United Nations estimates that on a vegetarian diet the world could support a population some six times greater than the present 5.2 billion. Just 4 hectares planted with soya beans can provide enough protein to feed 61 people for a lifetime; the same land used for beef production can feed 2 people.

## Fishing

Seafood makes up less than 5 per cent of the global diet but it is an important source of protein, particularly in developing countries. In 1951 the global fish harvest was 21 million tonnes. At that time the oceans were thought to be an unlimited resource, and fish catches rose by around 7 per cent each year until the mid-1970s.

**Right** *These people are starving because a severe drought has killed their crops.*

Japan now take more than two-thirds of the catch off the coast of West Africa.

## Industrialized farming

During the 1940s scientists began producing new seeds for farmers in the developed countries. These high-yielding seeds replaced lower-yielding traditional varieties. To make the most of the new seeds, large areas of land were drained and brought under cultivation for the first time. Many hedgerows were also removed to create larger fields more suited to mechanized farming.

The secret of the new seeds really lay in the way that they responded to irrigation, extra fertilizer and pesticides. At first, yields increased dramatically, doubling within the first 10 years. After that, farmers found they had to keep increasing the amount of chemicals they used to maintain the higher yields.

**Left** *A plane sprays pesticide on a crop of oil seed rape. The use of such chemicals has increased dramatically during the last 30 years.*

**Below** *The world's fish catch in 1986. Of the 35.7 million tonnes caught by ships from Asian countries, Japan accounted for 11 million tonnes.*

However, since 1975 catches have fallen slowly, reaching 87 million tonnes in 1986.

The combination of pollution in coastal waters and overfishing has led fishermen to go further, use finer nets and catch younger fish in order to stay in business. In doing so they know that fish stocks will continue to decline.

We have already overfished some species of whales and dolphins to the point of extinction or near extinction, and we are also taking far too many other fish from the northern oceans. For instance, North Atlantic halibut, cod and haddock stocks have been reduced by 90 per cent and herring by at least 40 per cent.

Nine developed countries now catch and sell one-third of the global catch for use in livestock feeds and fertilizers. What is more, having run down their own fisheries they now send fleets to exploit those of other nations. For example, fishing fleets from the USSR, Spain, Poland, France and

WORLD FISH CATCH, 1986

Total 87 million tonnes

million tonnes

40
35
30
25
20
15
10
5
0

Africa | North & Central America | South America | Asia | Europe | USSR | Oceania

Between 1961 and 1980 the developed nations doubled the amount of fertilizer they used; over the same period crop yields stayed more or less the same. Furthermore, the use of so many chemicals has created a range of problems for the environment. For example, around 70 per cent of our water supplies are now used for irrigation; this can only be achieved by taking water from underground sources faster than natural processes can replace it. We also know that in some countries much of the fertilizer used over the past 40 years is polluting groundwater supplies. Even if we stopped using artificial fertilizers today it would take many decades of rain to wash them away.

The use of pesticides has followed a similar pattern to that of fertilizers. At first they were seen as a miraculous tool. Later pests began to develop resistance to the pesticides. It also became clear that the chemicals stayed in the environment far longer than anyone had thought, killed wildlife and polluted water supplies.

Some farmers believe they have no choice but to find an alternative way to grow food that uses fewer chemicals, creates less pollution, and uses animals to restore soil fertility. This approach is now known as organic farming. Other, more technological, methods will also be tried to increase food production without harming the environment. Scientists are now attempting to use genetic engineering to develop crops that are resistant to pests and drought, need less water and make better use of soil fertility.

## The Green Revolution

After new seed varieties had been used successfully to increase agricultural yields in many developed countries, the same technology was exported to developing nations during the 1960s. This process was nicknamed the 'Green Revolution' and its main aims were to increase food production, reduce hunger and boost foreign trade.

Sure enough, in many areas high-yielding seed varieties increased production fourfold within 10 years. However, from environmental, economic and social viewpoints the Green Revolution proved to be a very mixed blessing. Each new irrigation scheme required the construction of a dam. Villages upstream of such a dam

*The countries shown as being 'extremely dependent' on fertilizers each use more than 150 kg per hectare on their arable fields every year.*

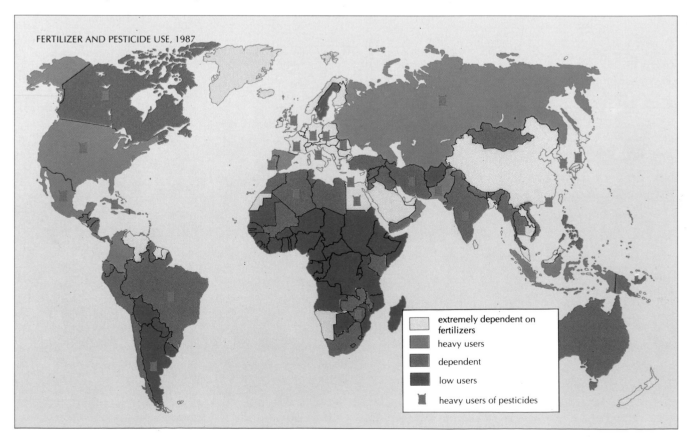

FERTILIZER AND PESTICIDE USE, 1987

extremely dependent on fertilizers

heavy users

dependent

low users

heavy users of pesticides

**Above** *This Japanese aid worker is helping farmers in Zambia to improve the way they grow food. The best form of aid is that which allows local people to help themselves.*

**Right** *One of the serious drawbacks to using large amounts of pesticides is that they can cause poisons to spread through the food chain. This black-headed gull has died as a result of taking in DDT, a highly toxic pesticide.*

were often completely destroyed and the people in them forced to move. In some places, irrigation has also led to an increase in the salinity, or salt content, of the soil. When this occurs, soil fertility is reduced dramatically, crop yields fall and soil erosion increases rapidly.

As in the developed world, it soon became clear that to keep their yields high farmers had to use more chemicals every year. However, many small farmers simply could not afford to buy ever-increasing quantities of expensive, imported seeds, fertilizers and pesticides. A large number of farmers got into debt, and their only means of survival was to sell their land to their richer neighbours and migrate to the cities to join the urban poor.

# DESERTIFICATION

Deserts occur naturally all over the world. The word 'desert' literally means a 'place that is deserted', although about 260 million people live in deserts or around their edges. We tend to associate deserts with very hot, very dry lands, covered with shifting sand dunes. A few deserts are like this, but most are made up of rock. Some, for example the Gobi Desert in central Asia, are actually very cold during the winter months, and even hot deserts are cold at night because there are no clouds to trap the heat of the day. Deserts cover over 12 per cent of the earth's land surface. Most occur around the tropics where the winds have passed over thousands of kilometres of land, or over high mountain ranges, losing all their moisture. Areas receiving less than 250 mm of rainfall per year are classed as deserts. Many receive far less than this and rain may not fall for many years.

**Right** *More than 12 per cent of the world's land is desert. The areas most at risk of desertification are on the edges of these natural deserts.*

*The small graphs show how the temperature and rainfall varies throughout the year in three desert areas.*

**Top right** *The Sahara Desert in Algeria. Not all deserts are hot and sandy like this part of the Sahara. Some, especially those at high altitudes, are very cold. Large areas of the Sahara and other deserts consist of rocks rather than sand dunes.*

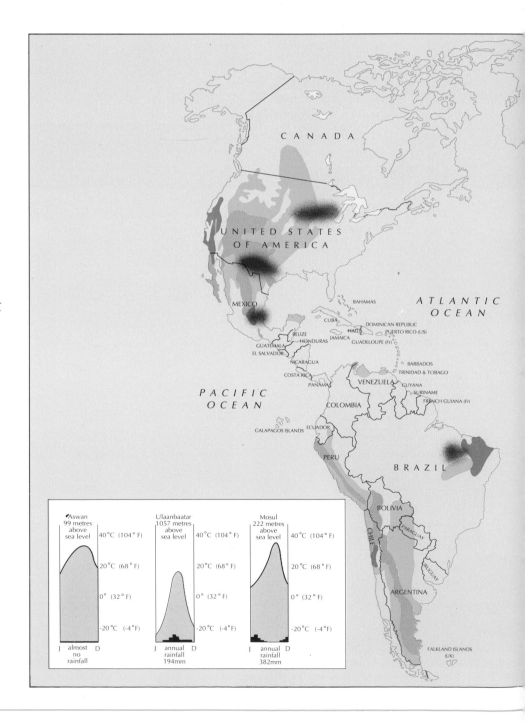

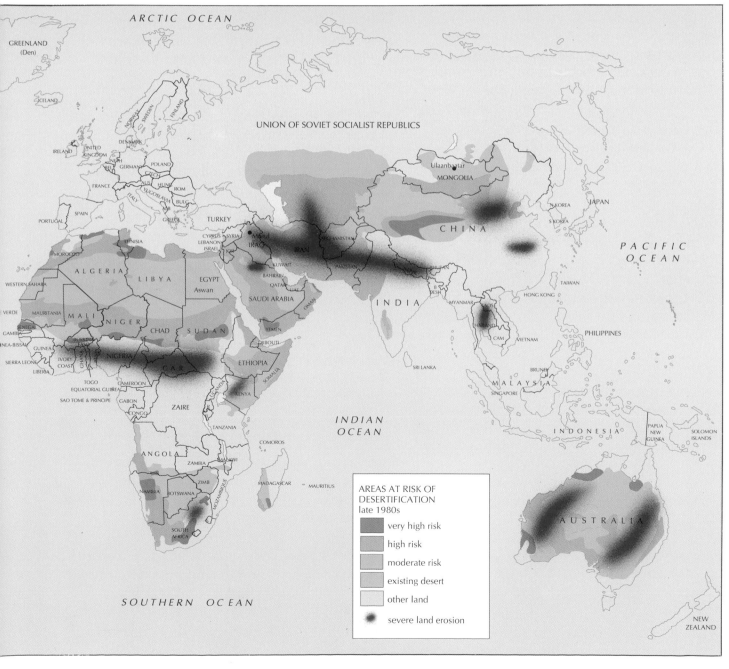

AREAS AT RISK OF
DESERTIFICATION
late 1980s

- very high risk
- high risk
- moderate risk
- existing desert
- other land
- severe land erosion

## Deserts on the move

Deserts are spreading, not naturally but as a result of the way land is treated by people. The areas most affected are those regions around true deserts, known as arid and semi-arid land. These areas receive between 250 and 600 mm of rainfall per year although most falls at one time of year, and in some years the rain fails. Although fertile, the soil is easily exhausted by too much cultivation or damaged when too many livestock – cattle, sheep and goats – are grazed on it.

Much of this land is made up of open woodland and scrub, as well as grassland. Collecting wood for fuel and overgrazing by goats now threaten much of that woodland. When too many trees are lost the exposed soil is easily eroded – washed or blown away – and so nothing can grow. This process, known as desertification, affects vast areas of land. It threatens millions of people with loss of their land, malnutrition, and often starvation.

## The causes of desertification

The spread of deserts is not caused by drought or even overpopulation, although both make it worse. The main cause is the way we manage, or mismanage, our land. Many different factors lead to desertification but it is important to understand that they are often inter-related and always far from simple.

Although it is often fertile, arid and semi-arid land contains little organic material, or humus. In the past, farmers allowed land to remain uncultivated, or fallow, for a period to allow it to regenerate. Alternatively they would co-operate with nomadic herders who grazed the land for a time; dung from their cattle and sheep fertilized the soil, and meat could be exchanged for the farmers' cereals.

In recent years increases in population and changes in traditional ways of life have put an end to such practices. In Niger, for example, the amount of grain harvested per hectare has decreased steadily over the last 50 years due to overcultivation and an increase in the production of cash crops. In the USA in the 1920s the traditional dry grazing lands of Texas, Kansas and Oklahoma were ploughed up to grow more

### Losing ground

● One-third of the earth's land surface is arid or semi-arid, supporting perhaps 600 million people. More than half this area is under direct threat of desertification.

● Every year 45 million hectares of land are affected by desertification and 6 to 10 million hectares completely lost to desert.

● It has been estimated that over 50 per cent of India's land is now suffering from varying degrees of soil erosion.

● The Sahel, a region to the south of the Sahara Desert in Africa, suffers the worst wind erosion of soil in the world.

● Soil erosion and desertification are not confined to the poorer regions of the world – although they are hardest hit by its effects. A larger area of land is affected in the USA, Canada and Mexico than on the entire African continent.

● Virtually the entire agricultural region of Australia is threatened by poor stock-raising techniques.

● In Asia at least 40 per cent of all land is at high risk of desertification; much of this is in the USSR.

● The cost of halting desertification world-wide is estimated at US$2.5 billion a year. The loss of output from the productive land which is lost to deserts each year is estimated at ten times this figure.

profitable wheat. But good cultivation methods were ignored and by the early 1930s the soil was exhausted and damaged by constant ploughing. Following two years of drought, a great storm in 1934 blew away 350 million tonnes of ruined soil and much of the American Midwest became a desert. Although the USA now has a national Soil Conservation Service, it is estimated that 40 per cent of American farms are still losing soil.

**Above** *The position of the fence in this picture shows where the level of the land used to be. Severe soil erosion has worn away more than 3 metres of soil.*

**Right** *This diagram shows who gets what percentage of the money we spend on a jar of coffee.*

All countries need exports to pay for goods they buy from other countries. They may earn money by growing cash crops, like tea, cotton or coffee, which other (usually richer) countries cannot or will not grow themselves. The problem is that cash crops are often grown at the expense of the food crops that would feed local people. During the famines in the Sahel in the 1970s, exports of groundnuts (peanuts) increased while local people died of starvation. In Mexico, 80 per cent of children in rural areas are undernourished while livestock – mainly cattle for export to North America – eat more grain than the entire human population of the country.

Cash crops are often grown on the best land, forcing small farmers to work for the cash crop companies, or to move on to poorer land. The crops are often unsuitable for the land, requiring constant treatment with expensive chemicals which damage

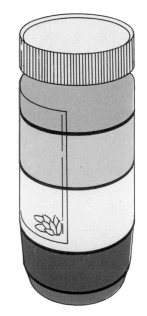

WHERE THE MONEY FOR A JAR OF COFFEE GOES

20% to shopkeeper or supermarket

25% to processors and wholesalers

28% to coffee traders and shippers

19% to country growing coffee

8% to farmer

the soil. Meanwhile the poorer land, now supporting too many people, turns to desert.

In dry areas the land is often more suitable for grazing animals on the sparse natural vegetation than for growing crops.

In the past, people keeping livestock herds were nomadic, moving frequently and spreading their herds widely, so preserving the grazing or rangelands. With increases in population and herd size, traditional grazing land is ploughed up for cultivation and the remaining rangeland soon becomes overgrazed and damaged further by trampling. The old migration routes of the nomads are also disturbed and the traditional co-operation between the herdsmen and the farmers breaks down.

In Senegal deep wells were bored to provide water for people and their livestock. The bore-holes attracted nomadic herders who no longer needed to move their cattle. Soon the land was overgrazed and the soil badly damaged for kilometres around the wells. In the USA more than half the rangelands owned by private farmers are overgrazed. Soil erosion has halved the possible grass production.

Nearly 90 per cent of people in poorer countries depend on wood as a building material and as a source of fuel. Much of this is collected locally from fallen branches or brushwood, but when this supply is gone trees are felled – and the dry woodlands begin to disappear. Demand from the growing cities is also immense and vast amounts of wood and charcoal are illegally trucked into towns and sold to those who can afford it. And, as populations increase, more and more woodland is cleared for agriculture, including cash crops.

Trees slow down heavy rain before it reaches the soil; their roots stabilize the soil, particularly on hillsides; and their falling leaves add to its fertility. Trees, literally, hold back deserts. Loss of forests in tropical countries such as Brazil and Malaysia creates desert-like soil conditions even though these are not arid areas.

According to United Nations estimates, more than 100 million people world-wide experience acute shortages of fuelwood. Women in Burkina Faso may have to walk for 4 to 6 hours several times a week to gather enough firewood to cook an evening meal.

*Overgrazing livestock on poor land is one of the main causes of desertification. This picture shows cattle in Nigeria.*

It may seem surprising that the irrigation of land, by digging wells or channelling water from elsewhere, can lead to desertification. But if irrigated land is not well drained, the land rapidly becomes waterlogged and the salts in the irrigation water build up, making the land useless for growing crops. Irrigation water may also draw up deeper groundwater with a high salt content. On the Indus plain of Pakistan, 2,500 square kilometres of farmland is now salt desert as a result of poor irrigation schemes. Too many wells may also have the effect of lowering the water table so that, eventually, all the wells become dry. Furthermore, we have already seen the effect that irrigation projects can have by attracting the nomadic herders.

So there are many complicated factors involved in the spread of deserts. Sometimes there is war within or between the countries involved, making life difficult for farmers and distribution of food impossible. Many of the poorer countries owe huge debts to the richer nations and have little money for their own development. Even if these debts are 'written off'

the countries are still tied by the need to sell cash crops, often at very low prices, or to accept 'aid' projects which may benefit the donor country more than the recipient.

Drought is a factor in the spread of deserts, and so is increasing population. But just as people can help to cause desertification, they can also be a factor, perhaps the major factor, in preventing it and turning back the spread of deserts.

*This boy in Rwanda is collecting wood to be used as fuel.*

## Stopping the spread of deserts

There are many ways in which land can be managed in order to reduce the effects of soil erosion by wind and rain. The methods used will depend on the particular situation, the local conditions and the materials available. They will only be successful when they are part of properly planned improvement programmes that involve the communities who will benefit from their success and tackle the underlying causes of desertification.

Cultivation methods can be improved so that more crops can be produced without damaging the soil. Drought-resistant crop varieties, like millet and sorghum, are already grown widely in arid countries. New crops such as grain amaranth and lima bean have also been shown to be very resistant to drought and, with an increase in the variety of crops grown, there is less likelihood of a total crop failure.

Higher production means that farmers are able to return to more traditional methods, such as crop rotation. A common four-year rotation is millet, cowpeas, groundnuts and a year of lying fallow.

Cowpeas provide fodder for cattle and also enrich the soil with nitrogen. Well-managed, usually small-scale, irrigation schemes can improve crop yields dramatically and can be used to establish small vegetable and fruit farms to improve the nutrition of local people.

The problems of overgrazing are perhaps more difficult to solve. In the past, the great grasslands of the world were grazed by wild herds, such as bison in the USA and saiga in the USSR. These were hunted almost to extinction and domestic animals, often unsuited to the conditions, took their place. Better disease control and research into hardier animals that are more like the original inhabitants of the grasslands, will improve meat production but may also lead to greater soil damage.

Tackling the problems of overgrazing does not necessarily mean a return to the 'old ways', but a combination of traditional methods and new techniques such as better breeding, disease control and better distribution. On the southern edges of the Koroli desert in Kenya, the Redille tribe lived in moveable camps, following their herds of sheep, goats and camels as they searched for the best grass. An attempt was made to settle the tribe in villages supplied by deep wells, but after several years of drought many of the tribe's livestock died. Now the Kenyan government is attempting to introduce the Redille back to a nomadic way of life, but this time providing many

small wells throughout the region and supplying other benefits and services associated with a settled way of life.

Stopping the loss of trees is perhaps the single most important act that would halt, and even turn back, the spread of deserts. Some trees can be grown which allow crop or livestock production to continue. The acacia is an example: it fertilizes the soil by adding nitrogen and phosphorus, its pods make nutritious animal feed, and crops such as millet can be grown underneath it. Later the wood can be used as a building material and for fuel.

Planting trees as shelter belts cuts down soil erosion by wind and rain. In the Indian state of Rajasthan, 1,500 km of roadside shelter belts have been planted, using trees that can be harvested for fodder and fuel wood. In one region of Niger, Africa, a windbreak scheme has increased cereal production by 15 per cent, while in another region it is hoped to produce 50,000 acacia, eucalyptus and orange seedlings a year to stabilize sand dunes and help restore agricultural land as a first step towards proper forest regeneration.

More efficient wood-burning stoves will reduce the amount of fuel wood required for cooking. If these can be locally and cheaply manufactured, like the United

*These are some of the ways in which desertification can be halted. Not all would be used in the same place.*

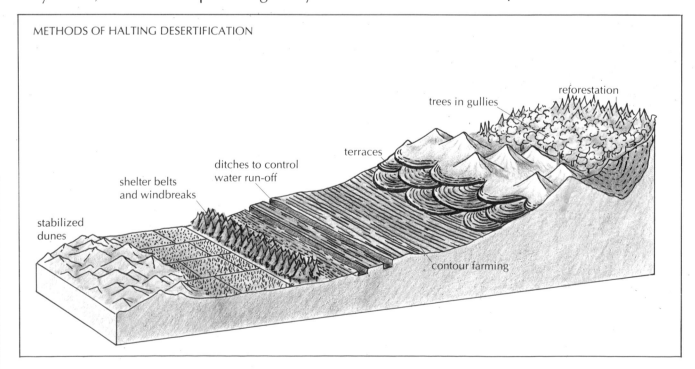

METHODS OF HALTING DESERTIFICATION

reforestation

trees in gullies

terraces

ditches to control water run-off

shelter belts and windbreaks

stabilized dunes

contour farming

introduced into 3,500 villages in the region.

In 1972 a small Oxfam experiment in Yatenga, Burkina Faso, began with the building of low, U-shaped earth walls to catch rainwater for tree seedlings planted inside them. The local people adapted the technique to help grow food crops, constructing low barriers of stones, stalks and branches across their fields to halt water run-off. Now the stone lines, or *diguettes*, have been built on over 5,000 hectares; a simple but effective technique has been devised to measure contours on the almost flat land so the *diguettes* can be sited correctly. There is now a constant stream of visitors to learn how it is done.

Both these examples may seen tiny compared to the areas affected by desertification world-wide. But they show what can be done when people understand the problem and are given the

**Above** *These plants are being grown to stabilize the sand dunes at the edge of the Sahara in Tunisia.*

**Right** *This desert area has been reclaimed. Crops can now be grown here in the shelter of the windbreaks around the field.*

Nations Environment Programme's 'Jiko' stove, success is more likely.

## Two success stories

In the Indian state of Gujarat a number of villages established plantations on communal grazing lands. Mixtures of seedlings for timber, fuel wood and fodder were supplied by the forestry department who worked closely with village councils. The villagers protected the plantations from grazing and fuel-wood poachers and, in return, shared in the profits when the trees were harvested. Now the scheme has been

tools to tackle it. Similar examples, both large and small, can be found throughout the world.

So desertification has little to do with droughts, too many people or bad luck. It has a lot to do with poverty, the relationship between the richer and poorer nations, and the way we all manage and use land. All? Yes, because many of our own decisions – what we buy, how much we are prepared to pay for it, even whether we bother to stick to the footpath rather than take the worn short-cut across the grass – affect the spread of deserts.

# ENERGY CRISIS

The world uses vast amounts of energy every year. Because we use it in many different forms – coal, gas, oil, electricity, wood-fuel and so on – we need a single yardstick to measure how much we are really using; this is the mtoe , or million tonnes of oil equivalent. It tells us how much energy we would use in a certain situation if it were in the form of oil.

We consume just over 9,000 mtoe each year, 78 per cent of it from fossil fuels. Oil itself provides about 34 per cent, coal about 25 per cent and natural gas about 19 per cent. The rest is made up of about 5 per cent from nuclear-generated electricity, 6 per cent from hydro-electricity (water power), and 11 per cent from biofuel and other sources such as solar, wind and geothermal power.

**Right** *This map shows the major reserves of the fossil fuels we use. The small graphs illustrate the size of the coal, oil and gas reserves in each region and the number of years they will last. The arrows show the movements of oil and gas around the world, from the areas that produce them to those where they are used. The thicker the arrow, the greater the amount of fuel moved.*

**Top right** *Energy use in the various regions of the world in 1989.*

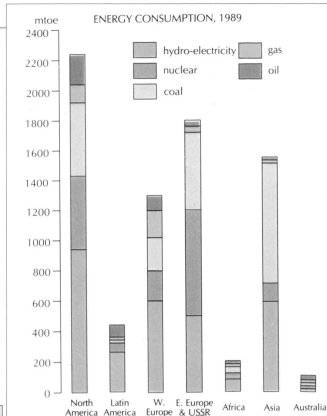

ENERGY CONSUMPTION, 1989

mtoe

hydro-electricity    gas
nuclear    oil
coal

North America, Latin America, W. Europe, E. Europe & USSR, Africa, Asia, Australia

## Who is using the energy?

The diagram (left) shows the energy consumption, in 1989, of the seven regions of the world, in the different sources of energy. Notice that the only figures we have are those for commercial fuels – wood and animal waste, for example, are not included – so the total for the developing countries, mainly in Africa, Latin America and most of Asia, is misleading.

Four regions – North America, Eastern Europe and the USSR, Western Europe, and Asia – take by far the bigger share. In Asia, the developed countries of Japan, South Korea and Taiwan account for over 33 per cent of the total, and China takes most of the rest. Clearly the parts of the world which are industrialized, developed

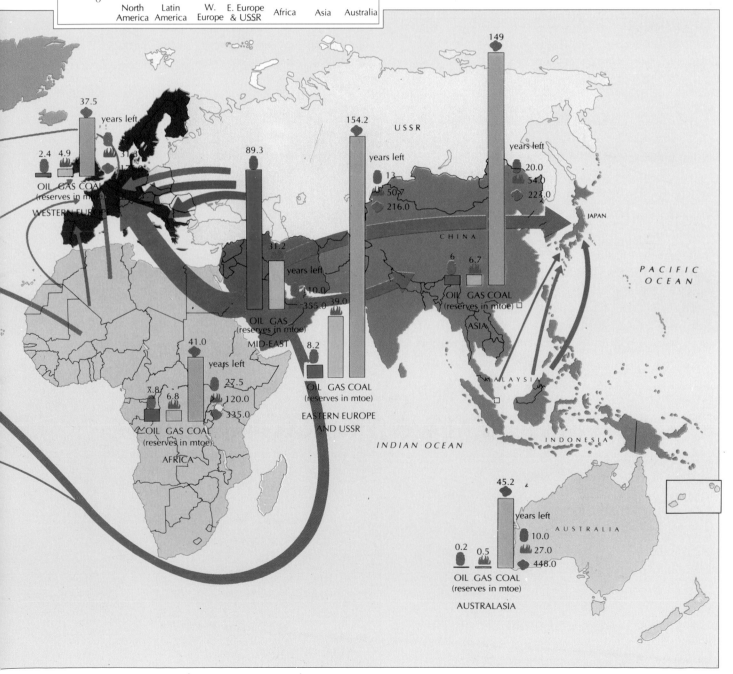

countries use more energy than the developing countries.

One of the reasons for this is that, in the developed world, most people are employed in industry, including manufacturing and service industries – in factories, shops and offices. Large amounts of energy are consumed in manufacturing processes, and in heating and lighting factories and office buildings. Developing countries have much less industry and so they consume much less energy in these ways.

Another reason why developed countries consume more energy than those in the developing world is to do with food. Although most people in developing countries work in agriculture, in the developed world agriculture consumes more energy. This is because farmers in developed countries use much more intensive methods – more machinery, artificial fertilizers and pesticides, which require energy both to make and to use. After leaving the farm the food is transported further and more energy is spent on processing it.

The third reason is transport. More than a

quarter of Britain's energy bill goes on fossil fuel for transport. In Britain, there are about 380 road vehicles per thousand people and in the USA the figures is 750. The figures for India and Indonesia are 2 and 15. It is a similar picture for air and rail transport. However, one form of transport which is used much more in developing countries is the bicycle. More bikes were bought in China in 1987 than there were cars bought in the whole world. China now has about 500 million bikes, and India 45 million.

The fourth major way in which people in the developed world use more energy is in heating their homes. This is partly because they are often in cooler climates and partly because they can afford a much higher degree of comfort. Although British homes have changed over the last 40 years to a more efficient way of heating – central heating rather than open fires – no less energy has been used for heat. People now

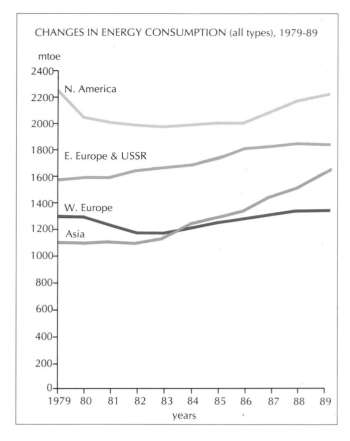

CHANGES IN ENERGY CONSUMPTION (all types), 1979-89

**Above** *Between 1979 and 1989, the change in how much energy we used varied from one region to another. This was partly due to the ways regions reacted to the sudden oil-price rise in 1978-1979.*

demand higher temperatures, they heat unused rooms, and are less careful about waste.

## Patterns of consumption

The diagram above shows how the consumption of energy in the four main regions changed between 1979 and 1989. The world price of oil rose sharply in 1978–79, and this led to an economic slowdown in many countries. In North America and Western Europe there were several years in which energy consumption did not increase and between 1979 and 1989 there was only a small rise overall. Yet Eastern Europe and the USSR and Asia increased their consumption significantly.

In part this is because Asia (apart from Japan) and Eastern Europe and the USSR were much less able than Canada, the USA and Western Europe to introduce energy-saving methods and equipment. It may not seem fair that the poorer you are, the less you are able to change things so that you spend less on energy, but it is true.

Another reason is that the Soviet-led communist systems that were then present in Eastern Europe and the USSR, fixed the price of energy way below the world price and so there was less reason to change the old, inefficient ways of using energy.

China – which uses over 40 per cent of Asia's energy – also has a communist system that kept the price of energy low and efficiency did not improve much. Asia also had a much bigger rise in population (as did Africa and Latin America) than the developed world, and more people use more energy. A further reason for Asia's rise in energy consumption between 1979 and 1989 was that Japan did much better, economically, than the rest of the world. This meant that it could afford both to find ways of using energy more efficiently and to use more energy altogether.

### Reserves

Reserves of fossil fuels, perhaps surprisingly, are constantly going up; not the real, actual fuel under the ground, but the 'proved reserves'. This term means the portion of the total actual reserves which we are reasonably certain we can extract, from known places, with today's technology and at today's prices. So, proved reserves go up if technology improves, enabling more to be extracted, and if the price goes up, making it more profitable to extract them. New discoveries also add to proved reserves.

There is still the problem that fossil fuels will run out eventually. Finding new reserves, like the oil and gas fields in the North Sea and Alaska, becomes more difficult all the time. But there are two other important problems.

Firstly, much of the world's fossil fuel reserves are in extremely inconvenient places. The Middle East, for example, has seen many wars in recent years, often with interference from outside the region, and these events can disrupt the extraction and transport of oil. The USSR, which produces 20 per cent of the world's oil, also has many problems – an economic crisis, a political crisis and a nationality crisis. These may lead to the break up of the Soviet empire which could have an unpredictable effect on the supply of oil.

The other major problem is not with future supply, but with possible future demand. One quarter of the world's population now accounts for 70 per cent of fossil fuel use. If the developing world were to start using fossil fuels at the rate of the developed world, the length of time that proved reserves are expected to last would be cut by 65 per cent. This change may be a 'fair' one, but it would be a disaster for energy supply.

However, the bigger disaster by far would not be to do with unburnt fossil fuels but with burnt ones – pollution.

### Pollution

The main pollutants from burning fossil fuels are carbon monoxide, carbon dioxide, sulphur dioxide, nitrogen oxide,

**Right** *An oil production platform in the North Sea. It is increasingly difficult to find major new reserves of oil because almost all of the most promising areas have already been explored.*

**Below** *Pollution produced by burning fossil fuels can damage people's health and disturb the ecological balance of the planet.*

particulates (minute particles of unburnt or partly burnt fuels) and ozone. There is also lead from petrol, and a wide range of toxic chemicals, such as benzene, which cause cancer.

Pollution from fossil fuels affects people's health, the trees and lakes, and the atmosphere of the whole globe. The health effects can be terrible. Carbon monoxide affects the ability of the blood to carry oxygen round the body. Sulphur dioxide and particulates cause lung disease, and lead attacks the nervous system. Ozone attacks the eyes and lungs. Pollution caused by fossil fuels is discussed in other chapters; for example, Chapter 7 explains the causes and effects of acid rain, while Chapter 9 covers the threat of global warming.

## The alternatives

If we are to cut down on the amount of fossil fuels we burn and reduce the level of pollution they cause, we must find other forms of energy to use. There are several possible alternatives.

Nuclear power: Although it costs a lot of energy to build a nuclear power station, once built it saves a great deal of fossil fuel and therefore reduces pollution. Today's nuclear stations prevent the atmosphere receiving 1 billion tonnes of carbon dioxide each year. There are also benefits in terms of reduced acid rain. Another benefit is that fewer people have been killed while working to produce nuclear power than in coal-mining.

However, the arguments against nuclear power have been getting stronger. Two major accidents – at Three Mile Island in the USA in 1979 and at Chernobyl in the USSR in 1986 – have made many people very concerned about safety. Disposing of the dangerous waste products from nuclear power is still an unsolved problem. The

radiation released from nuclear power stations into the air, soil and water is a great potential health hazard. Lastly, the costs of building and running nuclear power stations – and 'decommissioning' or closing them down when they become too old – are enormous.

Around the world, only 94 nuclear stations are currently being built – the lowest figure for 15 years. As old stations are shut down the total number in use may even reduce. To solve the fossil fuel problems by building nuclear stations, we would have to make some amazing savings on building costs, spend large sums of money on safety and find ways of disposing of the radioactive waste. Then, in order to make a big difference, we would have to build many hundreds at the same time.

Renewable energy: Energy from renewable sources is presently being used instead of fossil fuels which would otherwise put more than a billion tonnes of carbon dioxide into the atmosphere. This is less than the pollution savings with nuclear power, but renewable sources may be a better prospect in the long run, because they are much cheaper to build and to run,

*The shattered nuclear reactor at Chernobyl, after an explosion in 1986.*

*A windfarm in the USA. Electricity is produced by the spinning blades of the aerogenerators.*

excellent prospects for photovoltaics, which generate electricity directly from sunlight, and for solar power stations where solar rays are concentrated on to a hotspot to boil water and drive turbines that produce electricity.

Wind power: There are now 20,000 windmills generating electricity world-wide, mainly in the USA and Denmark. Britain has a small wind power programme, and in the future may have windfarms out at sea supplying some of the country's electricity needs.

Power from water: Many countries now have hydro-electric power stations, which use the energy of falling water to generate electricity. Tidal and wave power stations are also in operation. However, tidal power stations can have serious ecological effects, and wave power costs are uncertain.

Geothermal energy: The rocks below the earth's surface are hot and can be used as a source of energy. In some places, such as Iceland, hot water rises from the rocks to the surface and is used to heat homes and factories. In other parts of the world, water is pumped down to the rocks where it is heated and brought back to the surface. If the water is hot enough it can be used to generate electricity, and there are now geothermal power stations in eighteen countries.

and they are clean – no pollution is caused when a solar panel or a windmill is in use, and there are no waste products.

Solar power: All round the world, including Britain and other less sunny countries, solar panels could heat water for millions of buildings. Passive solar design – making sure that buildings receive the maximum energy direct from the sun – and good conservation measures could cut the pollution from heating buildings by 75 per cent.

In sunnier parts of the world there are

*Although many countries produce some of the energy they need from renewable sources, only a tiny proportion of the world's energy is made in this way.*

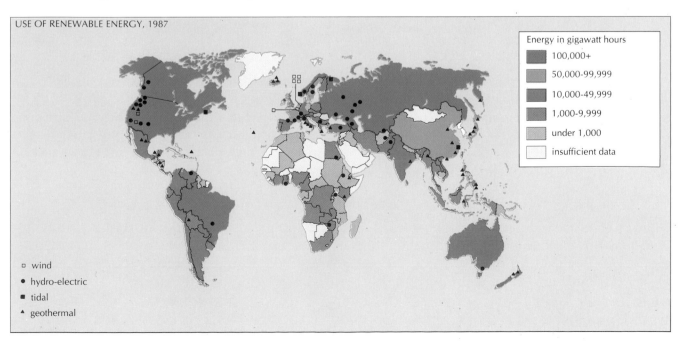

USE OF RENEWABLE ENERGY, 1987

Energy in gigawatt hours
- 100,000+
- 50,000-99,999
- 10,000-49,999
- 1,000-9,999
- under 1,000
- insufficient data

□ wind
● hydro-electric
■ tidal
▲ geothermal

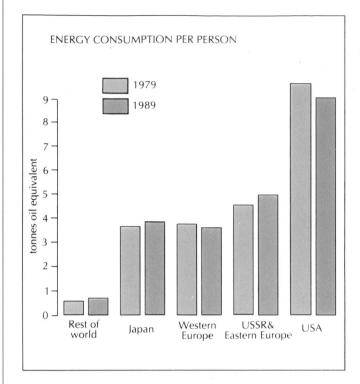

ENERGY CONSUMPTION PER PERSON

*Most energy is used in the developed countries of the world.*

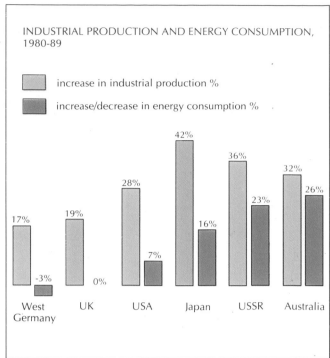

INDUSTRIAL PRODUCTION AND ENERGY CONSUMPTION, 1980-89

*A lot of the world's energy is used for industrial production.*

Biomass: Growing our fuel could bring a double benefit. If we grow more wood than we burn, the production of carbon dioxide is cut both while the trees are growing and when they are burned instead of fossil fuel. Burning the methane gas given off from rubbish dumps is also useful because unburnt methane is one of the gases that add to global warming. We could, of course, burn more of our rubbish to provide heat, but clearly we could not both burn it and recycle it!

## Using less energy

But the most important thing about all energy, whether or not it is renewable, is to use less of it.

We can use less energy in two main ways. One is by increasing efficiency – getting more light per kilowatt of power, or more kilometres per litre of petrol, for example. The other is conservation – devising methods of avoiding the need to use so much energy; for example, building houses that need less heating.

Since the big oil price increase of 1973, during the last Arab-Israeli war, the world has saved about $300,000,000,000 - worth of energy. The developed nations could save another 3 per cent per year, which would save the atmosphere another

4 billion tonnes of carbon by 2010.

The diagram above left shows how much energy is used per person in different regions of the world, and how this has changed since 1979. It is obvious where most of the energy is being used, and where and when the main improvements have come. The diagram above right takes into account the economies of the countries concerned. For each country there are two figures – the percentage increase in goods produced by that country's industries between 1980 and 1989, and the percentage increase in the country's energy consumption during the same period.

Efficiency: Different countries can have very different levels of efficiency in their use of energy in industry. One important way of increasing overall energy efficiency is to improve our industrial methods. Not long ago, a tonne of British steel cost three times as much energy to produce as a tonne of Japanese steel; Britain had always had cheap energy and Japan had not, so the Japanese had to be more efficient. However, Britain is now fast improving its methods of steel production and reducing the amount of energy used.

Transport: The world now has 500 million vehicles, producing a total of

550 million tonnes of carbon each year. There will almost certainly be a lot more cars around in the year 2010, producing much more pollution. However, if cars can be produced that use less fuel than today's models, the amount of pollution could actually fall.

The best way to save fuel and cut pollution would be to use fewer cars. Buses and trains give over six times as many kilometres per person per litre of fuel, even compared with an economical small car. Bicycles are far better still.

Lighting: This uses about 17 per cent of our electricity. We can cut that easily by using the new low-wattage bulbs. They use far less energy and also last longer. Fridges and other household equipment could be much more efficient; perhaps there should be tough standards for energy efficiency as there are for safety.

Electricity itself could be produced in a more efficient way in many places. A method known as Combined Heat and

*A traffic jam in Bangkok, Thailand. Cars and other vehicles use a lot of fuel and cause severe pollution problems.*

Power (CHP) is already in use in Britain and elsewhere, but we should make more use of it. In a normal coal- or oil-fired power station, 70 per cent of the heat from the fuel goes up the chimney into the air and is wasted. In a CHP station, it is used to heat water for houses, flats, factories, shopping centres, offices and so on – doubling the energy obtained from each tonne of fuel.

Heating: This is the form in which we use most of our energy, and it is an easy form to use less of. For example, the regulations for building houses in Britain were changed in 1990 to make new houses 20 per cent more energy efficient. This brings the British standard up to what the Swedish one was in 1932! It is technologically very simple, and quite cheap, to build heat-conserving houses. In 1978 the Centre for Alternative Technology at Machynlleth, Wales, built one which saves 90 per cent of the heat used in a normal house, at an extra cost of only 10 to 15 per cent on the price of the house.

We all have a choice to make: do we continue wasting energy, running down the world's fuel supplies and bringing on global warming, or do we change our ways?

# AIR POLLUTION

A layer of gases, water vapour and dust envelops the earth and supports life on it. It is called the atmosphere. Compared to the size of the earth, the layer is very thin: if the earth were shrunk to the size of a football, the atmosphere would be the thickness of a piece of clingfilm wrapped around it.
As well as providing the air that plants and animals need to stay alive, the atmosphere distributes moisture around the earth, prevents too much harmful solar radiation from reaching the surface and regulates temperature. However, by releasing smoke, fumes and other pollutants into the atmosphere, we risk damaging this protective, life-supporting layer.

## Air pollution - a world problem

Air pollution is not only found in areas where there are lots of factories. Once in the air, pollutants can be carried by the wind for several days and travel hundreds of kilometres. The environment in countries producing very little pollution can be damaged by pollution carried in the wind from other countries. Canada, for example, complains that much of the damage to its lakes and forests is caused by air pollution from the USA.

Burning fossil fuels for the energy they provide is the major cause of air pollution. The main pollutants are sulphur dioxide, nitrogen oxides, hydrocarbons and particulates (that is, particles of soot, dirt and unburnt fossil fuels). The highly industrialized countries use most of the world's energy and are responsible for most of the air pollution. Of the 100 million tonnes of sulphur dioxide put into the atmosphere every year, the USA is responsible for about 30 million.

So many countries are experiencing damage to their environment from air pollution that it has become a global problem requiring international solutions. International organizations like the United Nations Environment Programme and regional organizations such as the European Community are trying to persuade countries to agree on stronger air pollution controls.

## Acid rain

Air pollution is a major cause of acid rain. Fumes created when fossil fuels are burned are discharged into the atmosphere. Some fall to the ground quickly but

*In the past, acid rain affected mainly the countries of the developed world, but many developing countries are now beginning to suffer.*

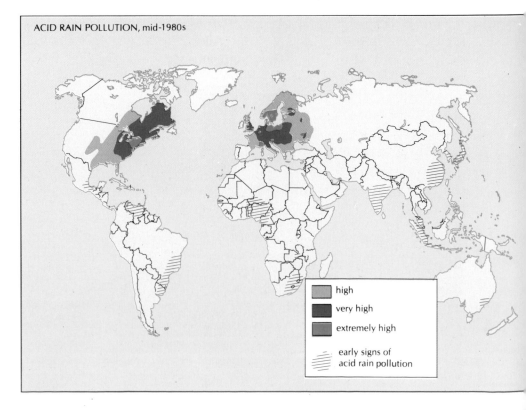

ACID RAIN POLLUTION, mid-1980s

high

very high

extremely high

early signs of
acid rain pollution

others, especially those from tall chimneys, are absorbed by moisture in the air. As a result of chemical changes they become weak acids. Eventually, the moisture returns to the earth as acid rain, often hundreds of kilometres away from the source of the pollution. Although called acid rain, it might fall as snow, mist or dew.

Acid rain can cause serious damage to the environment. If it falls where rocks and soils are alkaline, such as in chalk and limestone areas, the acid is neutralized and there is relatively little damage. If it falls where the rocks are acid, such as granite, the acid is not neutralized.

Large areas of Canada, Scandinavia and central Europe suffer a lot of damage because they have

*Another by-product of our overcrowded roads – noise pollution.*

acid rocks and lie down-wind of major industrial areas. However, acid rain is also becoming a problem in Venezuela, the east coast of Brazil, parts of West Africa, central India, eastern China, South Korea, Japan, Malaysia, Indonesia and eastern Australia. In fact, wherever there is industry there are signs of environmental damage from acid rain.

Although many animals and plants, including

*A diver photographs the only life still flourishing in a Swedish lake affected by acid rain – the carpet of blue-green algae that covers the lake-bed.*

deciduous trees, are affected by acid rain, coniferous trees and wildlife in lakes and rivers suffer most. Damage to coniferous trees can be recognized by yellow spots on the needles, fewer needles, dead branches at the top of the

tree and badly developed root systems which allow the trees to blow over more easily. In Czechoslovakia, 70 per cent of the forests are damaged by acid rain and, in some areas, hillsides that were once forested have become bare moorland.

Many of the plants and animals that live in lakes and rivers cannot survive if the water becomes too acid. Acid rain washes poisonous heavy metals like aluminium out of the soil and into watercourses where they harm living things. The number of fish and insects decreases until, in very acid lakes with a pH of around 4.5, there is little or no life. pH is the unit of measurement for acidity. pH7 is neutral, above 7 is alkaline and below 7 is acid. pH5 is ten times more acid than pH6 and 100 times more acid than pH7.

Buildings, too, can be damaged by acid rain. The rapid deterioration of the stonework on the Parthenon in Greece has been caused mainly by air pollution originating in the city of Athens.

The long-term solution to acid rain is to reduce air pollution. This can be done but it is costly and takes time. Sulphur dioxide is a major cause of acid rain. Power stations burning coal or oil are the main source. The amount of sulphur dioxide produced can be reduced by burning natural gas, which contains virtually no sulphur, burning coal or oil from sources which are naturally low in sulphur, or by removing the sulphur dioxide from the smoke before it reaches the atmosphere. Many countries have agreed to reduce the amount of sulphur dioxide they put into the atmosphere by 30 per cent before the end of the century. Countries seriously affected by acid rain say that a reduction of 80 per cent is needed.

In the short term there are some temporary solutions. Crushed limestone can be put into lakes or spread on the ground to help neutralize the acid rain. The main drawback is that areas need treating again after a few years, and the treatment is expensive.

*A layer of photochemical smog hangs over a town on the US-Mexican border. The smog is caused by the effects of sunlight on fossil fuel pollution.*

## Pollution from vehicles

By the year 2007, there should be no petrol or diesel vehicles on the roads in Los Angeles, USA. Only vehicles powered by electricity or cleaner fuels, such as ethanol, will be allowed. Air pollution in southern California is such a serious problem that drastic action is being taken. The authorities estimate that it will cost people about US$2.8 billion a year to make the changes, but this is small compared to the $13 billion cost of lower agricultural production and higher health bills resulting from air pollution.

Before 2007, other measures are likely to be introduced, including the outlawing of all free parking, enforcing car-sharing

schemes, and running all public and company vehicles on ethanol rather than petrol or diesel. These actions are needed in spite of the area having the strongest vehicle exhaust emission controls anywhere in the world.

Around the world there are over 500 million vehicles. Southern California, with 6 million, is not the only area facing terrible air pollution from vehicles, but it is one of the most active in trying to implement solutions. Road vehicles are a major source of air pollution in and around most cities. Thousands of vehicles are concentrated into a small area and the fumes enter the air at the same level as people are breathing and plants are growing. Between

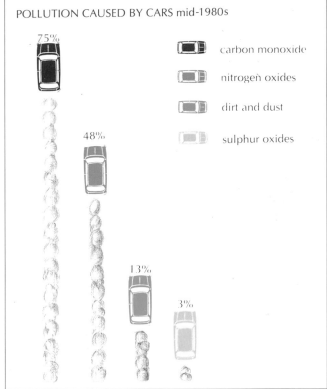

POLLUTION CAUSED BY CARS mid-1980s

75%

48%

13%

3%

carbon monoxide

nitrogen oxides

dirt and dust

sulphur oxides

**Above** *This diagram shows how much air pollution is caused by cars.*

the cities, major roads pollute the air of the rural areas as well.

In hot, sunny weather there is an additional problem. The pollutants react with the strong sunlight to form ozone. During the hottest part of the day, levels of this poisonous gas frequently exceed maximum recommended levels in many major cities and in the countryside around them. In some countries the weather forecast warns people when pollution levels are going to be high, so that old people, children and those with breathing or heart problems can stay inside.

### Cutting pollution

There are two ways to reduce the air pollution caused by motor vehicles. One is to reduce the amount of pollution coming from each vehicle, the other is to reduce the use of motor vehicles.

Today's vehicles use less fuel and produce less pollution than those produced as little as 10 years ago because of improvements to the design of the engines. However, the amount of traffic is increasing so rapidly that the total amount of pollution is not reducing. To curb pollution, many governments are introducing much stricter

**Above** *Some people wear masks to try to keep out the poisonous fumes of city traffic.*

controls. For example, all new cars for sale in the European Community after 31 December 1992 will have to be fitted with a catalytic converter. This small device, fitted to the exhaust of the car, removes most of the carbon monoxide, nitrogen oxides and hydrocarbons which cause pollution. However, it does not remove carbon dioxide, one of the major causes of global warming. The exhaust fumes from diesel engines, too, will have to be much cleaner.

Lead, which is added to petrol to improve an engine's performance, ends up in the air along with the other pollutants. It is poisonous and very dangerous for young children. Petrol companies have steadily reduced the amount of lead in leaded petrol. Most cars on the road today can use unleaded petrol. Catalytic converters will only work on cars which use unleaded petrol.

Drivers could help reduce pollution by sometimes choosing to go by public transport, running smaller cars and driving more smoothly and more slowly. A recent survey in Britain revealed that although people realized their vehicle was a major cause of pollution, they were unwilling to give it up or drive more slowly!

Reducing pollution from individual vehicles is unlikely to reduce air pollution in the long term because more and more vehicles are being used. Improved public transport would persuade some people to leave their cars at home, but regulations are likely to be needed to tackle the problem effectively. In Athens, for example, cars with even-number and odd-number registrations are allowed into the city centre on alternate days.

**Air quality in urban areas**
Air pollution is worst in large cities where there are many buildings, factories and vehicles in a small area. The pollutants enter the air in such quantities that they are not diluted to safe levels by the air. Much of the pollution comes from burning fossil fuels to provide the energy for heating buildings, powering vehicles and machines, generating electricity and making things. But the air is polluted by many other chemicals as well, some of which are poisonous and very damaging if they become too concentrated in the air. The cloud of gas that escaped in 1984 when there was an accident at a factory in Bhopal, India, killed 2,000 people living nearby.

The industrial cities of Britain were once notorious for their vile-smelling winter smogs – a mixture of fog and smoke from burning coal. Even in the middle of the day

conditions are aggravated by air pollution and the occurrences of these diseases are much higher in industrial towns than in rural areas. However, air pollution in the cities of Eastern Europe and newly industrializing nations like China or Mexico are much worse. There are fewer controls because the equipment needed to reduce pollution is expensive. With poverty and unemployment the highest priorities, governments are reluctant to impose expensive controls on industry.

## Action to reduce pollution

People and governments are now much more aware of the importance of clean air for all living things and the dangers of continuing to pollute the atmosphere. We

**Above** *The chimney of a wood-pulp factory belches out pollution into the air.*

**Right** *Demonstrators in Budapest, Hungary, protest about air pollution. The countries of Eastern Europe have severe pollution problems.*

it was sometimes not possible to see more than a few metres. Following a particularly bad smog in London in 1952, when the death-rate increased from 250 to 1,000 people per day, action was taken. The Clean Air Act of 1956 created smokeless zones in which smokeless fuels like coke, oil and gas had to be used. The air now looks much cleaner and the so-called 'pea-soup' smogs are a feature of the past. Most of the highly industrialized nations now have similar laws to try and keep the air in the cities clean.

Although most industrialized countries have pollution control laws, the problems still exist. Asthma, bronchitis and heart

need to use the earth's resources to improve our lives, but at the same time we must not damage the earth that provides these resources.

The problem has been recognized but there are no simple or cheap answers. Progress is being made on reducing air pollution. The leading industrial nations have agreed to reduce sulphur dioxide emissions from large industrial works and the major pollutants from vehicle exhausts. New pollution control technologies are being developed and industry is being encouraged to use them according to the principle of using the 'best available technology not entailing excessive cost'.

# POLLUTED WATERS

Almost every day rivers, lakes, seas and oceans are being polluted. On
television and in newspapers, there are frequent reports of oil disasters,
pollution by toxic chemicals and damage caused by acid rain. In many places,
untreated or partially treated sewage is being pumped into the sea, causing
severe pollution. This is particularly true around the Mediterranean, and it has
serious consequences for the tourist industry and the local population.
All of these problems are threatening to damage one of our most precious
resources – the water we all need to live – and to disturb the ecological
balance of our planet.

**Below** *All over the world, rivers, lakes and
seas are being polluted with a wide range of
domestic, industrial and agricultural wastes.*

*Out in the oceans, ships dump their waste
oil and tanker accidents produce vast oil
slicks that kill marine plants and animals.*

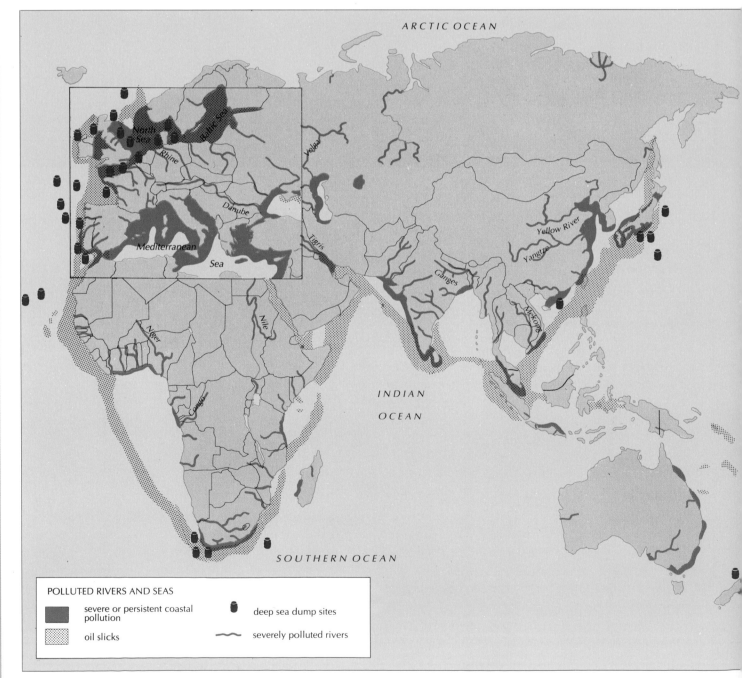

POLLUTED RIVERS AND SEAS

- severe or persistent coastal pollution
- oil slicks
- deep sea dump sites
- severely polluted rivers

## Our drinking water

The oceans cover about 70 per cent of the surface of the earth, and contain a vast quantity of salt water. Only 3 per cent of the water on the earth's surface is fresh water. Fresh water is essential to life on earth – plants, humans and other animals depend on it for their survival.

Most of the world's fresh water can be found in the frozen polar ice caps and mountain glaciers. The air also contains fresh water, in the form of vapour, and the

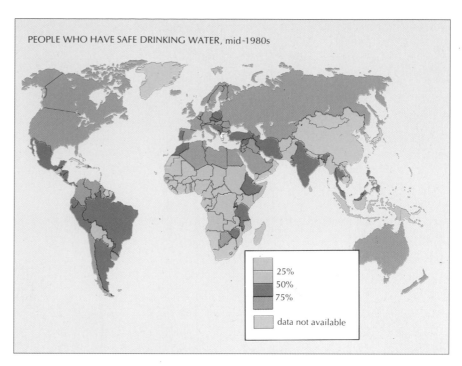

PEOPLE WHO HAVE SAFE DRINKING WATER, mid-1980s

25%
50%
75%

data not available

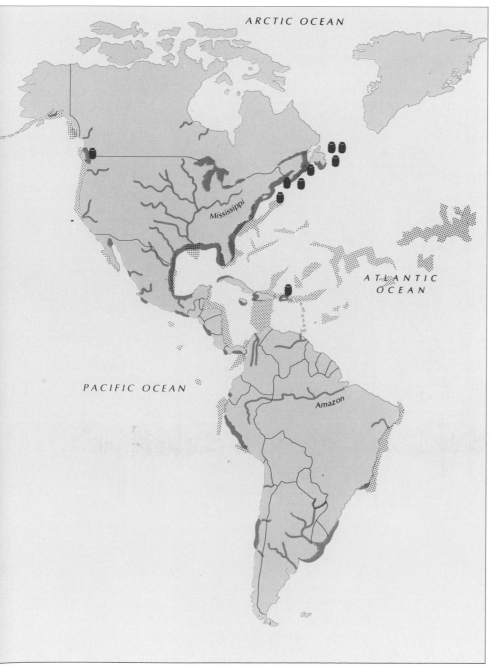

**Above** *In many developing countries, only a small proportion of the population has access to clean drinking water. In India, 97 per cent of the available water is used in farming and industry.*

rest lies on or under the earth's surface – in lakes, rivers and ponds or as groundwater in the rocks and soil beneath our feet.

Fresh water is essential to our drinking water supply, and as the world's population increases so does the demand for clean drinking water. Because of environmental pollution, it is increasingly difficult to maintain our supply of good drinking water. The pumping of industrial waste into rivers means that many chemicals find their way into the environment, and into reservoirs from which our supplies of drinking water are taken. As a result, more and more compli- cated equipment and techniques are required for water purification.

### The polluted Rhine

The River Rhine is sometimes called Europe's largest open sewer pipe, because serious leakages and dumping of industrial and domestic waste are frequent occurrences. Tens of millions of people depend on the Rhine for their drinking water. Following an explosion and fire at the Sandoz chemicals plant in Basle, Switzerland, in 1986, a large quantity of toxic substances leaked into the Rhine. Millions of fish died as a result, and the supply of drinking water from parts of the river had to be stopped.

In many parts of the world, polluted rivers carry dangerous substances and deposit them in seas and oceans. Many of these substances, including heavy metals such as mercury and cadmium, pesticides and PCBs, sink down to the mud on the sea-bed. Micro-organisms such as water-fleas and shrimps that feed near the sea-bed, take in these poisons. They are then eaten by small fish which are, in turn, eaten by larger fish. In this way, the poisonous substances are passed up the food chain.

This can also be dangerous to humans, because poisons such as PCBs are not broken down in the bodies of fish. When the fish are caught and eaten by humans, the poisons are again passed along the food chain. In some countries, including Japan and Taiwan, people have been poisoned by PCBs. Many countries have now laid down rules governing the use of PCBs, but these are not always followed. In several developing countries and in Eastern Europe, very high concentrations have been found in the drinking water.

Obtaining clean drinking water in the developing world is a big problem. Many developing nations are in parts of the world where drought is a serious threat. Furthermore, the water that is available is often polluted by untreated sewage that has been pumped directly into rivers and lakes. Bacteria in the polluted water can cause dangerous diseases in people, including cholera. The careless use of fertilizers and pesticides is also responsible for the pollution of drinking water. The World Health Organization (WHO) attempts to help people in many developing countries to dig wells for

drinking water. They are finding that more and more of the water underground is polluted by agricultural chemicals.

### Radioactive pollution

The use of nuclear energy, particularly for generating electricity, has resulted in radioactive waste being allowed to enter the seas and oceans. Radiation has been found to be highly dangerous, and can cause serious diseases, including cancers.

Many tests on nuclear weapons have been carried out in the Pacific Ocean. In Micronesia, an area with more than 1,000 islands, over 50 nuclear tests have been carried out since the 1950s. Many islands have been discovered to be contaminated with radioactivity, and scientists have found that many plants and animals have been affected. Many of the islanders are also suffering from illnesses caused by exposure to radioactivity. Some children have been born with deformities or have died within a few days of birth. France is still carrying out nuclear test explosions on the island of Mururoa. The environmental group Greenpeace has campaigned strongly against the tests, but with little success.

Another problem is the dumping of radioactive waste material into the oceans. Radioactive waste is sealed inside concrete containers which are then dumped from ships into the oceans. But nobody knows how long the containers will remain sealed. If one leaks, radioactivity could contaminate seawater, with incalculable consequences. A large number of countries have now agreed not to dump nuclear waste into the oceans. Nowadays it is often

**Left** *Villagers in southern India collect their water from the only source of supply – the village pipe.*

**Right** *A chemicals plant pumps polluted water into the sea on the coast of Humberside, England. In the past, many industries regarded seas and rivers as free dumping grounds for their waste.*

stored on land, in old mine workings or in specially constructed storage facilities.

The leakage of radioactive waste water from nuclear power stations and processing plants is also a threat. Faults have occurred at the plant in Sellafield, England, where used nuclear fuel is reprocessed so that some of it can be re-used. As a result, an area of 3,000 square kilometres in the Irish Sea has been polluted with radioactivity. Some scientists believe that children whose fathers work at Sellafield are more likely than other children to suffer from leukaemia, a type of cancer.

### Greenpeace in action

Greenpeace was founded in 1970 in Vancouver, Canada. Its first actions, in 1972 and 1973, were directed against the nuclear tests carried out by the USA under the island of Amchitka, in the North Pacific Ocean. They made the headlines around the world. Since then, Greenpeace has grown from a small group of volunteers to an international environmental organization with representatives in many countries, including Canada, the USA, France, the Netherlands, Germany, Britain, Denmark, Australia and New Zealand.

With its ship, *Sirius*, Greenpeace regularly tries to stop the dumping of chemical and radioactive wastes. The group also campaigns to protect sea mammals, including whales. A number of whale species are threatened with extinction as a result of overfishing, and Greenpeace is fighting to have commercial whaling banned throughout the world.

In 1990 Greenpeace took action against the use of drift-nets. These are fishing nets which have a very fine mesh. Widely used by some Asian countries, such as Japan, Taiwan and the Philippines, drift-nets can be up to 50 km long. They are suspended in the water, forming 'walls of death' which trap all but the very smallest sea creatures. They are usually designed to catch tuna fish, but many other fish, seals and dolphins also become entangled in them. Greenpeace estimates that as many as 100,000 dolphins are killed each year by being caught in drift-nets.

In many parts of the world, the oceans' fish stocks are being reduced by pollution and by overfishing – catching fish when they are still very young and before they have been able to breed. Some fishing grounds have almost been emptied of fish. People are now beginning to realize how much damage is being done. But even if immediate steps are taken to solve the problems, it will be a long time before the ecological balance is restored.

### Coastal pollution

The coastal seas around densely populated industrial areas are especially at risk from pollution. In the waters off New York and Tokyo, and in the Irish Sea, countless fish are killed by pollution caused by industrial and domestic wastes dumped in the sea. In these and other areas, fish and shellfish can become so contaminated that they cannot safely be eaten by humans. Mussels caught off New York, Rio de Janeiro and Minamata (in Japan), for example, have been found to contain dangerous levels of heavy metals. Mercury – one of the most lethal heavy metals – poisoned more than 2,200 people in Minamata in the 1970s. The mercury

**Above** *Members of the environmental group Greenpeace protest against waste dumping at sea.*

**Left** *Overfishing and sea pollution have seriously reduced the stocks of many species of fish.*

had accumulated in their bodies because they had eaten fish and shellfish that were contaminated by pollution from a chemicals plant.

The Baltic Sea, between Scandinavia, the Baltic countries and Germany, is the largest area of brackish water in the world. Brackish water is a mixture of salt and fresh, and so saltwater and freshwater creatures live side by side. More than 150 million people live around the Baltic and they dump vast amounts of pollution into the sea from their homes and industries. As a result, the Baltic has become seriously polluted, especially by untreated sewage,

agricultural chemicals and oil. Baltic fishermen frequently haul up in their nets drums of poison gas, and ammunition that contains lead, dating from the Second World War. Many of the drums have corroded, allowing the dangerous gas to enter the seawater. This has had a devastating effect on the environment. Some fish caught in the Baltic are deformed, with a misshapen backbone, two heads or tails, or swellings on their bodies. In 1974 the Helsinki Convention, made up of countries surrounding the Baltic, agreed to reduce the amount of pollution they allowed to flow into the sea.

The North Sea, between Britain and continental Europe is home to many marine plants and animals. Rivers flowing into the North Sea carry a great deal of pollution. The countries around the North Sea have drawn up many environmental treaties and regulations to reduce pollution, but these have not been successful so far.

**Left** *This bird has been coated in oil following the* Exxon Valdez *disaster in 1989, when an oil supertanker ran aground on the coast of Alaska.*

**Below** *As a huge slick spreads out from the* Exxon Valdez, *another vessel attempts to pump some of the remaining oil from the damaged ship.*

In the North Sea there are about 350 oil-drilling platforms. Accidents occur regularly, causing large quantities of oil to escape into the sea. Many ships carry cargoes of toxic chemicals across the North Sea, and there have been shipping accidents in which these chemicals have leaked into the water. Some merchant ships flush out their oil tanks into the sea. Although special aircraft are used to detect such deliberate oil spills, their task is a difficult one, especially at night. Many ports now have depots to collect waste oil from ships. Hopefully, less waste oil will find its way into the sea.

The Mediterranean is an inland sea between Europe and Africa. The water is often seriously polluted because many areas around the Mediterranean pump their sewage directly into it. This is a problem particularly in major tourist areas, such as Spain and Italy, and many beaches are heavily polluted. Holiday-makers can find themselves swimming in water with a high concentration of sewage, which can cause stomach infections and

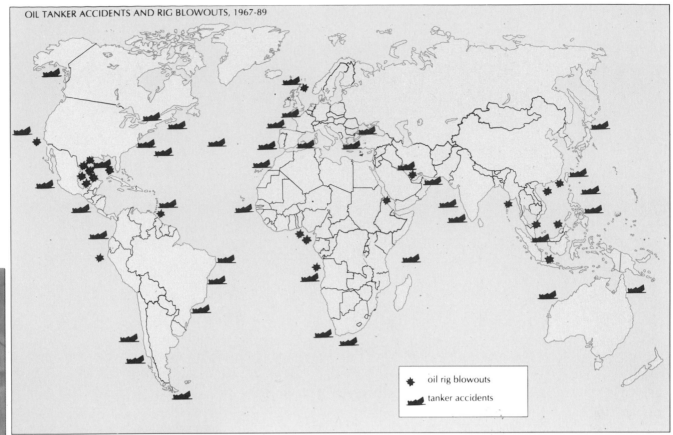

OIL TANKER ACCIDENTS AND RIG BLOWOUTS, 1967-89

★ oil rig blowouts

🚢 tanker accidents

more serious health problems.

Many industrial plants release chemicals into the Mediterranean. In some areas 80 per cent of the fish caught suffer from cancer and other diseases. This is a result of contamination by phosphates, PCBs, heavy metals and pesticides.

## Oil disasters

Oil spills from tankers, drilling platforms and pipelines can cause huge environmental disasters, polluting coasts and killing vast numbers of sea birds and other animals. Along the Dutch North Sea coast alone, more than 40,000 birds die each year from oil pollution.

In March 1989, the supertanker *Exxon Valdez* ran aground in the Prince William Sound, Alaska, spilling more than 45 million litres of crude oil.

*The* Exxon Valdez *disaster was the largest of many tanker accidents. Oil rig blowouts add yet more oil pollution to the oceans.*

Because of bad weather and the low temperature of the water, it was almost impossible to clear up the oil, and over 1,700 km of shoreline was heavily polluted. The damage to the environment was made much worse because the clean-up operation was very slow, and as a result the fishing communities around Prince William Sound suffered an enormous blow.

During the Gulf War in 1991, one of the world's largest oil pollution disasters occurred in the Arabian Gulf. Clean-up operations were more difficult even than in the *Exxon Valdez* spill, because the slick was in a war-zone.

## Coral reefs

Coral reefs are unique underwater ecosystems. They occur in warm, shallow tropical seas, and consist of tiny living creatures packed together side by side. When coral creatures die, new ones grow on top of them, and so the reef gradually becomes larger.

The Great Barrier Reef, off the east coast of Australia, is the largest coral reef in the world. It extends over 2,000 km, and is home to hundreds of thousands of plants and animals, from microscopic plankton to small fish and large sharks, each of which has its place in the ecosystem. All of these plants and animals can thrive only so long as the balance of the ecosystem is maintained. If the balance is disrupted – by pollution, for example – irreparable damage can be done.

Reefs in many parts of the world are now threatened by pollution, oil-drilling operations, the development of tourist resorts, and by divers collecting shells and corals. In order to protect these stunningly beautiful areas, environmental organizations are hoping to have them designated as underwater nature reserves, rather like those that already exist on land.

## Phosphates

In recent years, phosphates have been widely used in detergents and fabric softeners. When they are flushed down the drain with the used washing water, phosphates can find their way into rivers and streams. In these environments they may cause a huge increase in the growth of algae. The algae uses up all the oxygen in the water, and so many fish die. Phosphates reaching the sea can cause large 'blooms' of algae to develop in the water, killing marine plants and animals, and irritating the skin of people bathing.

**Left** *Coral reefs are home to countless living creatures. They form very delicate ecosystems which are easily destroyed by pollution and other human activities.*

**Below** *This river is so heavily polluted that nothing can live in it except the algae which covers the surface.*

More and more washing powders are now being manufactured with less or no phosphates – an important step in the right direction. But this solves only a small part of the problem. Phosphates are also found in much greater quantities in other products, especially fertilizers.

In some countries, so much agricultural fertilizer is spread on the land that significant quantities find their way into rivers and the rocks below the surface. Drinking water supplies can become contaminated as a result, putting people's health at risk.

The Netherlands alone produces about 95 million tonnes of fertilizer each year. Because of the damage caused to the environment, the Dutch authorities have drawn up strict rules governing its use. Although this is a problem in many parts of the world, as yet very few other countries have begun to tackle it.

# CLIMATE UNDER THREAT

As we have seen, the earth is surrounded by a thin layer of gases, water vapour and dust, called the atmosphere. This layer acts like the glass in a greenhouse, which allows sunlight in but prevents heat escaping quickly. Without the earth's atmosphere the average temperature of the planet would be about -18°C, which is too cold for most living things to survive.

However, what seems to be happening now is that the earth is becoming too hot. It is believed that certain gases that the modern world releases into the atmosphere are trapping too much of the earth's heat. These gases are known as greenhouse gases. The warming of the earth, which most scientists now believe is occurring, is known as global warming.

Global warming will have a major effect on where we live, what food we eat and how we work. Scientists are warning that over the next century we could experience changes in wind and rainfall patterns, crop yields, growing seasons, the level of water in oceans and lakes, and the distribution of plants and animals.

The world needs to plan for different weather conditions in the next century and cut down on the emission of greenhouse gases immediately.

*As a result of global warming, the climate in some areas will become drier while other regions will become wetter. This map is shaded to show how regions would be affected if the amount of carbon dioxide in the atmosphere were twice its present level. The symbols show where the effects of these climatic changes would occur.*

*If the earth's atmosphere were to heat up by even a few degrees, the Antarctic ice cap would begin to melt and the sea-level would rise. Many low-lying coastal areas would vanish beneath the sea.*

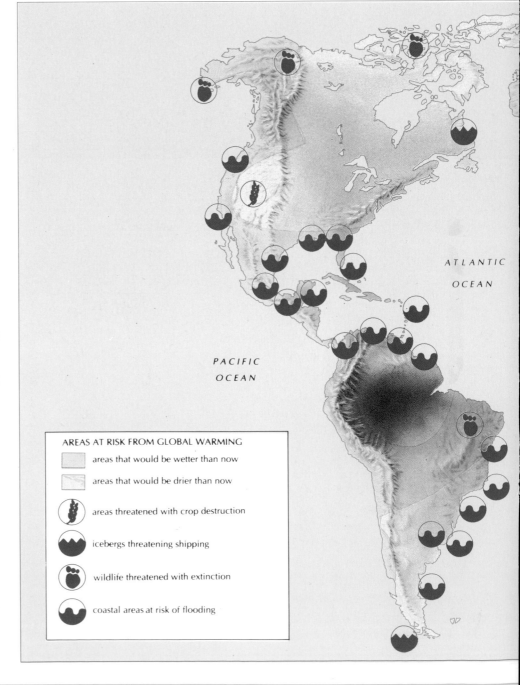

AREAS AT RISK FROM GLOBAL WARMING

- areas that would be wetter than now
- areas that would be drier than now
- areas threatened with crop destruction
- icebergs threatening shipping
- wildlife threatened with extinction
- coastal areas at risk of flooding

## How the earth is warming

Since the Industrial Revolution of the eighteenth and nineteenth centuries, many nations have built pollution-producing factories and cut down forests to make way for farmland and cities. The result is that there is now 25 per cent more carbon dioxide, methane and nitrogen oxide in the atmosphere. Unlike naturally occurring oxygen and nitrogen, these gases absorb infra-red radiation from the sun and this leads to more heat in the atmosphere. As the temperature rises, the warmer air is able to store more moisture in the form of

**Left** *Freak storms occasionally cause severe flooding in low-lying coastal areas.*

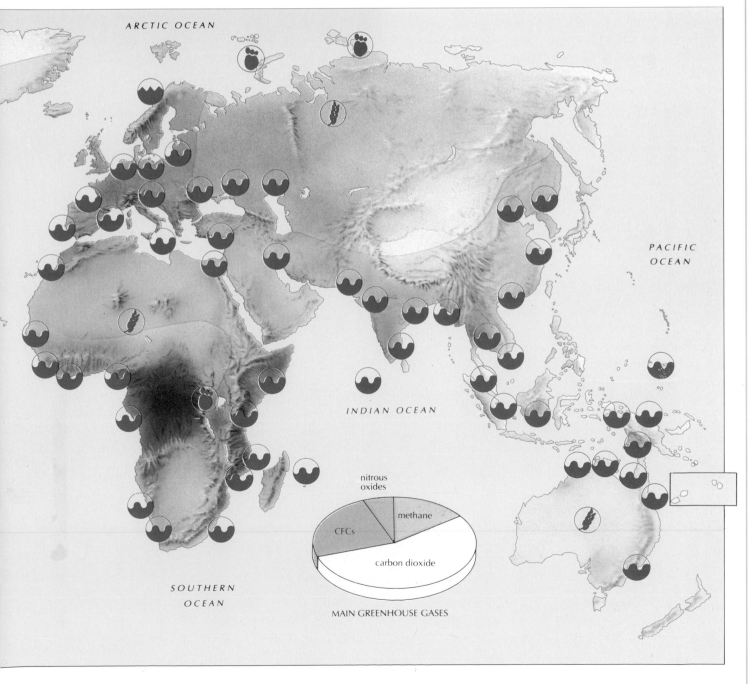

MAIN GREENHOUSE GASES

water vapour, which further increases global warming by preventing even more heat escaping from the atmosphere.

Although the average temperature has risen and fallen during this century, scientists have calculated that it has risen about 0·5° C since 1900. During the 1980s there were 6 years of record temperatures, followed by 1990, the warmest year on record.

Sophisticated computers are now being used to try and predict how temperatures might change in the future. In 1990 the world's top experts reported to the United Nations Environment Programme that they estimate the average global temperature will rise 1·3° C by 2030 and 3° C by 2070. The increase will be greatest closer to the poles because greenhouse gases are more concentrated there.

**Below** *Indian villagers protect themselves from the monsoon rain.*

### Climatic conditions

All the weather we experience is the result of air movement. As the sun's rays heat the earth, the air above it is warmed. This warm air rises creating an area of lower pressure below, which is in turn filled by cooler air. This continuous movement of air creates the winds. As the warm air rises it collects moisture from plants and bodies of water such as rivers, lakes and seas. The air cools as it rises, and is able to hold less moisture, and the excess moisture falls as rain, snow or another type of precipitation.

Violent winds and rain can occur in the form of tropical cyclones – also known as hurricanes or typhoons – which occur between 5° and 20° north and south of the Equator, where the sea temperature is

**Above** *A satellite picture of Hurricane Gilbert, which began in the Caribbean in September 1988.*

**Left** *A farmer in the Midwest of the USA surveys his withered crops. This area has suffered several periods of severe drought in recent years.*

warm and the earth's spin creates strong currents in the air. Pushed along by trade winds, hurricanes generally travel westward and often strike population centres such as the Caribbean and southern USA, India and South-east Asia. As the temperature of the sea rises due to global warming, hurricanes may occur further from the Equator but as yet scientists do not know this for certain.

## The changing climate

The weather we experience can be altered by natural climatic changes, events in outer space, and by human activities. In the Indian region of Rajasthan rainfall has become unreliable, and many scientists believe this is a direct result of farmers having cut down vast areas of forest. The dry air currents that rise above the ground can no longer pick up additional moisture from the trees and so less rain falls in the region. In contrast, vegetated areas help warm, moist air to rise and this enables greater rainfall to reach food crops further inland. Some scientists believe weather can

be affected hundreds of kilometres from a deforested region. They have shown that rainfall in tropical forests helps to release natural gases into the upper atmosphere. These elements are thought to help make rainfall occur in other parts of the planet. One computer prediction states that destroying the Amazon rainforest would reduce rainfall by 20 per cent and contribute several degrees to global warming.

It seems certain that global warming will change the climatic conditions of the earth but no one is sure precisely what the changes will be. Undoubtedly warmer air will cause the Antarctic ice cap to begin melting and the level of the oceans will rise, causing some coastal areas to become flooded. It may be that rainfall in temperate zones will increase by 5 to 10 per cent but this is difficult to predict accurately because of other factors. For example, short-term variations in the earth's orbit and the brightness of the sun can change rainfall patterns and the violence of storms. Slight shifts in the earth's tilt, called nutation, can change seasonal temperatures. In the 1990s faster computers and increasing knowledge gained through research will help scientists to develop a more precise picture of climate changes that will occur due to global warming.

## Damage to the atmosphere

Human-made elements released into the atmosphere can lead to a series of problems that threaten our climate, as in the case of global warming. However, substances such as chlorofluorocarbons (CFCs) have another, more devastating and immediate effect – the reduction of a form of oxygen, called ozone, in the atmosphere. Ozone is one of the gases in the atmosphere that protects the earth from the harmful radiation produced by the sun. Without this protective filter, ultraviolet,

gamma and cosmic radiation would disrupt the healthy formation of plant and animal cells on earth. We see the effects of receiving too much ultraviolet radiation when we stay in strong sunlight for too long – we get sunburnt.

Ozone breaks down easily when it reacts with certain other chemicals, such as CFCs. These chemicals have been in common use for many years – as propellants to push ingredients out of aerosol cans, as coolants in refrigerators and air conditioners, and in the manufacture of expanded polystyrene foam. Only 20 years ago, CFCs were

**Below** *Much of Bangladesh would be drowned by a 1-metre rise in sea-level.*

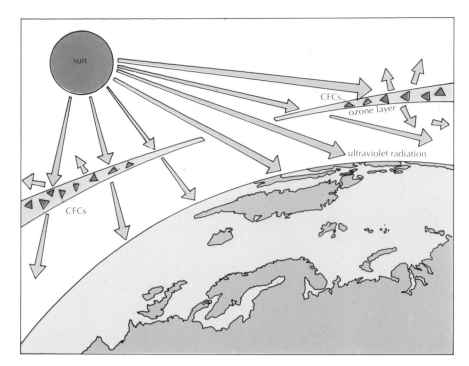

**Left** *CFCs are broken apart by the sun's rays, producing chlorine atoms. These atoms react with ozone and make still more chlorine. As this continues, more and more ozone is destroyed.*

**Below** *Concorde in flight. This supersonic plane contributes in a small way to ozone depletion by adding to the amount of chlorine in the atmosphere.*

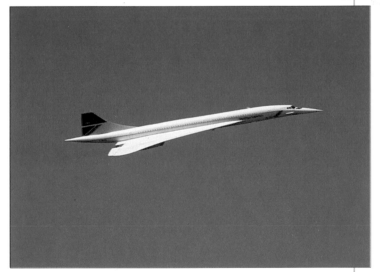

regarded as wonder substances that were non-flammable, non-toxic, easy to store and chemically stable.

This view changed in the 1970s when British, Canadian and American scientists realized that CFCs pose a major threat precisely because they are so stable. As they do not break down, CFCs float unchanged in the atmosphere, rising steadily for about 8 years until they reach the ozone layer. Finally they are broken apart by massive amounts of ultraviolet radiation. As they break down, the CFCs release millions of chlorine atoms which cause chemical reactions that pull apart the molecules of ozone. The chlorine atoms do not change after each reaction, and one atom can go on to destroy 100,000 ozone molecules. The result is a steady depletion of our protective layer of ozone.

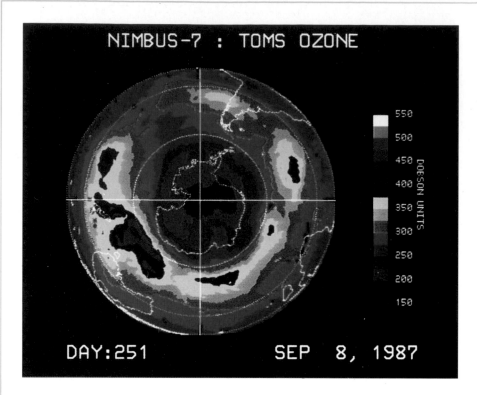

NIMBUS-7 : TOMS OZONE

550
500
450
400
DOBSON UNITS
350
300
250
200
150

DAY:251            SEP  8, 1987

*A satellite picture taken in 1987 of the 'hole' in the ozone layer above the Antarctic. As more CFCs drift upward through the atmosphere, more ozone will be destroyed.*

## Holes in the ozone layer

In 1982 a British team working at Halley Bay in the Antarctic discovered that atmospheric ozone was severely reduced in the area. This became known as the 'Antarctic Hole'. In truth this is not yet an actual hole but a large 'slice' out of the protective layer, particularly noticeable at lower altitudes. Later studies found that this 'hole' is as deep as Mt. Everest and as big as the USA or a large part of Europe.

Since1982, scientists have been using satellites, ground sensors and even modified high-flying spy planes to discover the cause of the 'hole'. They have found that high concentrations of chlorine atoms, mainly caused by CFCs, are to blame. Because of unique wind patterns and other factors, the ozone layer above Antarctica is particularly sensitive to the build-up of chlorine. However, it has recently been discovered that the ozone layer above North America, Europe and Asia is also reduced, and parts of South America, New Zealand and Australia have suffered ozone reductions of up to 20 per cent. As a general rule, it seems that the further a country is from the Equator the greater it is at risk from ozone depletion.

With more ultraviolet radiation hitting earth there will be more cases of skin cancer, which already kills over 100,000 people each year. Our immune systems will also be affected, making it more difficult for us to fight diseases, and increased radiation reaching our eyes will lead to more people suffering from cataracts. An even more serious threat is the possibility that food crops on land and plankton in the sea will be killed. Without these first links in the food chain the delicate balance of life could be destroyed.

## Solving the problem

Global warming, climate change and ozone depletion affect the whole world, so it is important that any solutions involve all national governments. Often the United Nations acts as a source for international co-operation.

In 1987 an international agreement called the Montreal Protocol was signed by 81 countries, promising to limit the production of CFCs. However, the problem of the destruction of the ozone layer was so serious that 3 years later the nations met again and agreed to speed up their efforts: by the year 2000 no CFCs should be produced. Other ozone destroyers, including halon, carbon tetrachloride and methyl chloroform, will also be phased out.

It will take many years for the ozone layer to recover, because the CFCs we sprayed out in 1984 or 1985 are only now reaching the upper atmosphere. Nonetheless, international action may have been taken in time to avert a catastrophe and this gives us hope for action on other issues in the 1990s. Many nations are now prepared to tackle global warming and to produce a world treaty on the climate in the 1990s. Environmentalists hope that United Nations members will give more money to environmental research programmes in this decade.

## Hope for the future

Human beings can be destructive but we can also be remarkably inventive. We are developing new technology to generate power from sources that do not contribute to global warming, including solar, wind, water and geothermal energy. More households and businesses are becoming concerned about energy wastage, and re-use and recycling programmes are now operating in many parts of the world. Plans for the 1990s include recycling plastics, reducing paper usage and developing better insulated glass windows. As people have shown that they are concerned about environmental problems, governments have reacted with plans to help us organize for a cleaner world in the next century.

**Right** *At this plant the CFCs which are used as a coolant in refrigerators can be removed safely, preventing them from entering the atmosphere.*

**Below** *Although most CFCs have been produced and used in the developed countries, the depletion of the ozone layer will affect countries throughout the world.*

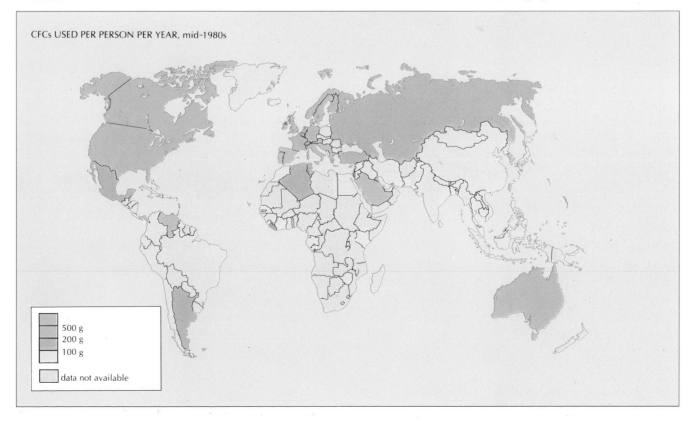

CFCs USED PER PERSON PER YEAR, mid-1980s

500 g
200 g
100 g
data not available

# CONSERVING OUR WORLD

Modern technology has given humans the means to exploit the earth's natural resources more than ever before but, although it has improved the standard of living for some people in the world, the environmental costs have been high. Many wild areas of the world have been destroyed by development such as building, mining, forestry and agriculture and by pollution of the land, water and air.

The situation is serious but not hopeless. Many steps are being taken to change and improve the environment. Some of them are international, such as the 1987 Montreal Protocol to limit CFC gases entering the atmosphere; others are national projects, such as the plant-a-tree day in China. Action must be taken by governments and by industries, but a lot can also be done at a local level – by everyone in their everyday lives. Environmental problems are caused by ordinary people doing ordinary things. We can all help to solve the problems by changing some of the things we do.

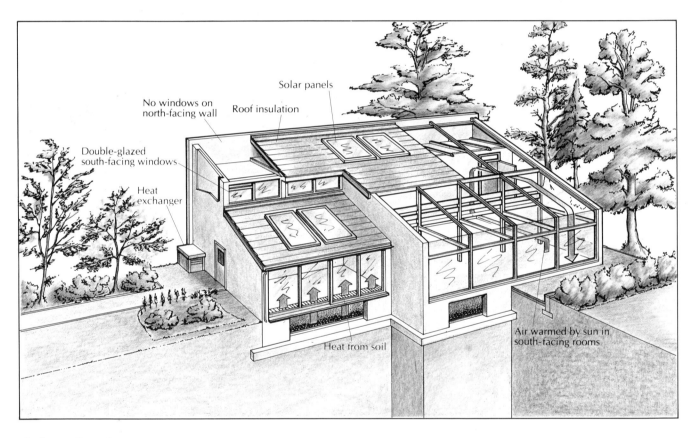

Labels: Solar panels · No windows on north-facing wall · Roof insulation · Double-glazed south-facing windows · Heat exchanger · Heat from soil · Air warmed by sun in south-facing rooms

## Saving energy

Using energy wisely is one of the most beneficial actions we can take because energy use is at the cornerstone of our lifestyles. We do not use energy just for heating, cooking and lighting but also for transport, and running factories and offices.

Being more efficient in the ways we use energy can have an immediate effect on carbon dioxide pollution. For example, between 1973 and 1987, American industries and transport improved their energy efficiency by 26 per cent. This meant that carbon emissions stayed at

*Energy usage could be cut by using 'passive solar design' in new homes. This means building them to take maximum advantage of the sun's energy.*

1.2 million tonnes a year rather than increasing. Huge energy savings could be made if public transport and bicycles were used instead of cars, and many countries such as the Netherlands and the USA are now improving their 'mass-transit' systems.

In the home, insulation and double glazing can reduce energy consumption and many countries now have minimum

**Above** *A geothermal power station in Kenya.*

**Right** *Bottle banks are becoming an increasingly common sight in many countries. The glass is collected and made into new bottles and jars.*

because energy is needed to make all these products.

One effective way of using less is to cut down on waste. An American chemicals company, Dow, has set up a 'Waste Reduction Always Pays' (WRAP) programme. It aims to reduce the amount of waste entering the environment and to save the company money. In 1960, Dow created 1 kilogram of waste for every kilogram of product it manufactured. By the 1980s, the company had reduced its waste to one-thousandth of that amount.

It is not only industries that can save resources. Households throw out huge amounts of paper, cans, bottles, plastic and food. Many of these can be recycled so that the materials can be re-used – glass, can and paper banks are now found in many towns. In Sydney, Australia, the local council has set up a recycling service which collects glass and paper from houses every week. Many recycling plants are opening up all over the world. The most technically advanced plant in the USA is at Rhode Island where 168 tonnes of newsprint and 210 tonnes of mixed rubbish are processed each day. The plant can recycle some types of plastic bottles as well as aluminium, glass and tin cans.

Recycling has a promising future – everyone can reduce their own waste and take recyclable materials to their local recycling centre. It is also important to re-use and repair things rather than throw

insulation standards for any new home that is built. Low-energy long-life light bulbs, energy-efficient washing machines and fuel-saving vehicles are all now available in the shops.

Using less energy is the most important way of saving resources and reducing pollution but the development of renewable energy sources, such as solar, wind, geothermal and water power, is also vital for the future. Solar collectors are now a source of hot water in several countries, including Israel; the Philippines and New Zealand use geothermal and hydro-electric power as major energy sources; and California has 'wind farms' where windmills generate over 1,000 megawatts of electricity.

### Conserving resources

Using less of everything is another 'green' alternative – less water, less food, fewer consumer products such as televisions, cars and so on. This helps us to use less energy

**Left** *Waste plastics being compressed into bales prior to recycling.*

them away and to buy fewer disposable products. Less waste costs less money and creates less pollution.

**Preventing pollution**
Developing cleaner machines and technologies can also make a big difference. Over recent years, concern over the 'hole' in the ozone layer has led manufacturers to phase out the polluting CFC gases they used as propellants in aerosols and

**Right** *This map shows just a small number of the species facing extinction; in total, there may be as many as one million. In the past, environmentalists were mainly concerned about the loss of animal species. However, each plant species may support up to forty animal species, and if the plant becomes extinct so do the animals. As the graph shows, the rate at which species are dying out is increasing dramatically.*

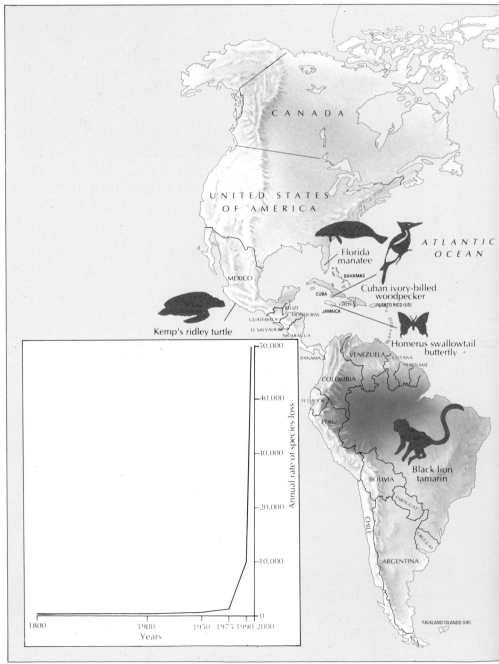

to replace them with other gases or with pump-action containers. Many other industries are following suit and are looking for ways to clean up their production processes.

In shops and supermarkets, more and more 'environment friendly' household products are being sold. These include biodegradable washing powder and washing-up liquid, organic garden fertilizer and rechargeable batteries. So by choosing carefully what we buy, all of us can help the environment.

For many years, environmental pressure groups such as Friends of the Earth (FoE) have campaigned to alert people to what they are doing to the environment. One campaign urged people not to buy

products containing hardwoods from tropical forests, and asked them to write to politicians, decision-makers and businesses about deforestation. In recent years their hard work has paid off as green issues have become prominent in many countries.

The increase in public concern about the environment has influenced political parties and many now claim to have green policies. Furthermore, many countries have recently introduced protection laws.

## Humans and other animals

Since life first began, many animal and plant species have disappeared from the earth. This is called extinction. It is a natural part of evolution and it has happened to millions of species. But the rate of

Barn owl
UK / Denmark / Germany

Tobias' caddis fly

Chinese alligator

Baiji dolphin
China

Mountain gorilla
Central Africa

African elephant
Central / E. Africa

Orang-utan

Javan rhinoceros

Rock wallaby

Tasmanian freshwater limpet

Eucalyptus carnabyi

Blue whale
S. Atlantic

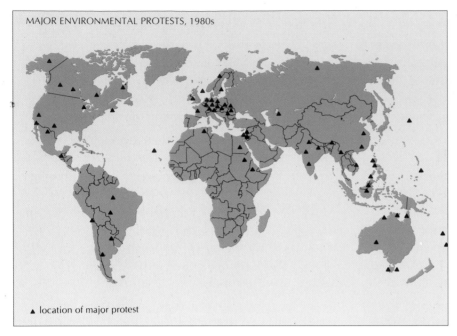

MAJOR ENVIRONMENTAL PROTESTS, 1980s

▲ location of major protest

**Left** *Throughout the world there have been many major protests against environmental problems such as water and air pollution, acid rain, deforestation and nuclear power.*

**Below** *A collection tank for waste oil.*

extinction is increasing, and it is a matter of concern that many species become extinct, or are endangered, because of human activity. The most famous example is the dodo. These large, flightless birds once lived on the island of Mauritius, in the Indian Ocean. In the 1600s settlers arrived on the island and hunted the dodos. They also introduced dogs, cats and rats which ate the dodos' eggs and chicks. By the 1700s there were no dodos left.

### Why conserve wildlife?

Plants and animals on the earth depend on each other to live. Humans are animals, too, although we often forget this, and we also depend on other species for the basics of life such as food, shelter, clothing, medicines, and so on. It is in our own interest to look after other species. Contact with nature is also a source of pleasure and wonder to humans, and many artists and scientists have found inspiration in the natural world.

### Causes of extinction

The main causes of species becoming extinct or endangered are hunting, loss of habitat, pollution and destruction by other species which have been introduced either deliberately or accidentally. Hunting was responsible for the near-extinction of the American bison and the Arabian oryx, although both have been saved by captive breeding and reintroduction programmes. More recently the plight of rhinos in Africa

has hit the headlines. They have been ruthlessly hunted for their horns and the population has been reduced by 70 per cent. Animals are often hunted to produce luxury goods, such as reptile skin shoes, fur coats and ivory carvings.

The destruction of habitats is a major threat to species. Land is taken for agriculture, mining or forestry, or may be lost because of soil erosion or desertification. Development projects can also disrupt the natural territories or migration routes of species. Tropical forests are particularly at risk because they are such rich ecosystems. They are home to more than half of all known species, but they are disappearing at an alarming rate. The creation of protected areas, such as nature reserves and national parks, can help counterbalance this loss of habitats.

Pollution can also endanger species. For example, oil spilled from tankers affects marine life such as fish, whales and other marine mammals and sea birds.

## Which species are threatened?

Thousands of animals and plants around the world are threatened with extinction. We usually only hear about the 'famous' threatened species – large mammals such as the giant panda and the African elephant. But most endangered species are little-known insects, reptiles, birds and plants. There are, for example, over 1,000 threatened mollusc species, and in the plant world it is estimated that over 25,000 species are endangered.

Some humans are also threatened. Tribal peoples are often vulnerable. In the sixteenth century there were over 5 million Indians living in the Brazil region of South America; today only 250,000 remain and they are constantly under threat from mining and forestry operations.

programmes are run by many organizations world-wide.

Captive breeding programmes can save species from extinction. The Hawaiian goose was reduced to a total population of less than 50 birds in the 1950s when the naturalist Sir Peter Scott took a few birds back to the Wildfowl Trust in Britain. The geese bred in captivity and there are now over 1,000 – and more than 200 have been reintroduced to their homeland. This method is now being used to help other species whose numbers have been greatly reduced in recent years, including the African black rhino.

Laws are another way of protecting animals and plants. Over 80 countries have signed the Convention on International Trade in Endangered Species (CITES). CITES aims to stop the trade in threatened species and products made from them. The European Community (EC) also has very strict regulations on the import and export of wild animals and plants, and licences have to be obtained before species can be taken to or from member countries.

**Left** *Since 1980 the number of black rhinos in Africa has fallen from 15,000 to under 9,000 because of poaching.*

**Below** *The Australian rock wallaby is under threat of extinction.*

## What is being done?

Accurate information about threatened species is vital, and one organization, the World Conservation Union, is monitoring the state of species in the world. It has data on over 30,000 endangered species at its Conservation Monitoring Centre in Cambridge, England, and publishes the Red Data Books which list those species at risk. Spreading the conservation message is essential and environmental education

**Going, going . . .**
• There are between 5 and 8 million different species in the world; only 1.6 million have been identified.
• Over 1,000 large mammals and over 25,000 plants are threatened or endangered. It is estimated that between 40,000 and 60,000 plant species will disappear during the next 50 years.
• Trade is banned in about 675 endangered species and regulated for another 27,000 species.
• The legal trade in wildlife is worth US$5 billion per year; the illegal trade is worth US$2 billion.

**Right** *A marine iguana basks in the sun on the Galapagos Islands. Many species on these islands are found nowhere else in the world.*

## Unique areas of the world

To protect wildlife and their habitats and to conserve wild and beautiful places, many locations around the world have been declared 'protected areas'. The first ever protected area was the Yellowstone National Park in the USA, which was set up in 1872. Since then many countries have established nature reserves and national parks. Some have been set up to protect the habitat of one important species, for example, the Wulong Reserve in China aims to conserve the giant panda. Other areas are established to ensure that a unique landscape, such as the Great Barrier Reef in Australia, is not damaged.

Some protected areas have to be international, because wildlife does not know about national boundaries and frequently crosses over them. Reserves often need to be 'transboundary', such as the German-Luxembourg Nature Park.

There are also reserves administered by international organizations:

**Biosphere reserves** are selected because they contain a complete ecosystem rather than any one individual species. The aim is to set up reserves covering all the types of ecosystem in the world. There are over 200 sites listed and many more proposed.

**World Heritage Sites** are sites which qualify as areas of 'outstanding universal value'. They are set up by UNESCO under the World Heritage Convention and countries which sign the Convention are allowed to suggest sites. To become a World Heritage Site an area must have either examples of major stages of the earth's evolutionary history, examples of geological processes or biological evolution,

**Below** *Some of the world's major protected areas, including World Heritage Sites, Ramsar Sites, biosphere reserves and national parks.*

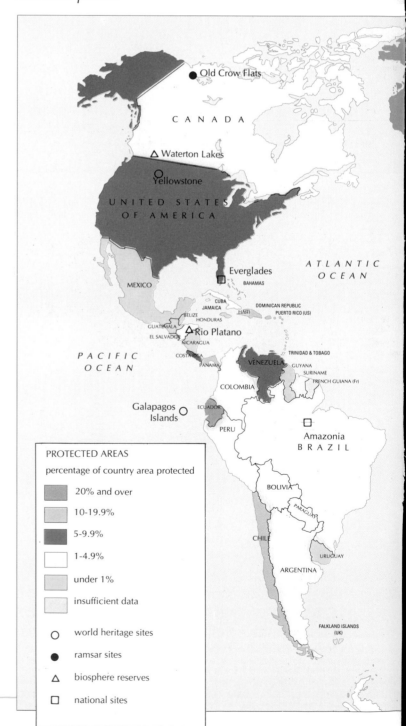

PROTECTED AREAS

percentage of country area protected

- 20% and over
- 10-19.9%
- 5-9.9%
- 1-4.9%
- under 1%
- insufficient data

○ world heritage sites
● ramsar sites
△ biosphere reserves
□ national sites

rare or outstanding natural scenery, or rare or endangered species of plant or animal.

**Ramsar Sites**. Wetlands, including coastal marshes, river estuaries and mangrove swamps, are very important habitats, especially for many species of birds. The conservation of wetlands was given an international dimension in 1971 when the Convention on Wetlands of International Importance especially as Waterfowl Habitat was established at Ramsar, Iran. In 1990 the Convention had been agreed by 52 countries and between them they had listed 445 protected sites covering nearly 30 million hectares. This network of protected wetlands is vital to the survival of many plant and animal species.

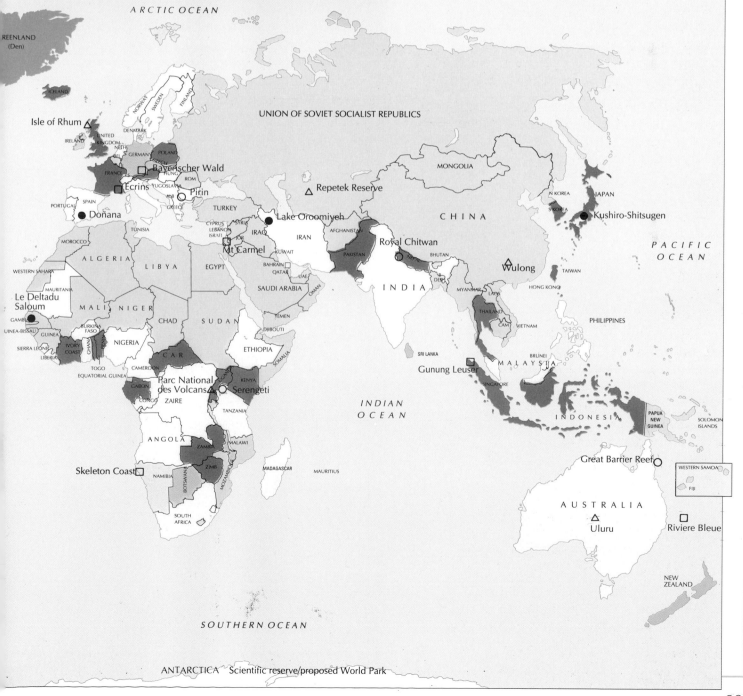

**European Community Special Protection Areas (SPAs)** are protected areas for birds in the countries of the European Community (EC). The EC proposes a network of sites in its Directive on the Conservation of Wild Birds, and stresses the need to conserve all birds and their habitats.

**World Park Antarctica.** Antarctica is a special place in the world. It belongs to no country but is covered by the Antarctic Treaty of 1959 which states that the continent is for 'free and non-political scientific research in the interest of all mankind'. Many countries now want to start mining operations in Antarctica and do not want the treaty to continue in its present form.

In 1972 a group of conservationists called for Antarctica to be designated a World Park but this cannot happen unless the idea is supported by most countries of the

*Greenpeace has called for Antarctica to be made a World Park, to protect the continent from mining and other human interference.*

world. The environmental group Greenpeace has been campaigning for World Park Antarctica so that this unique wilderness will be protected for ever.

### Strategies for survival

Making laws is an effective method of protecting the environment and many countries now have strict laws and regulations on pollution control, wildlife protection, waste management and energy conservation. There are also international laws, treaties and conventions to deal with problems such as dumping waste at sea, pollution of the atmosphere and trade in wildlife.

In 1980, the first ever global approach to the world's environment was launched by the United Nations, the World Wildlife Fund (now called the World Wide Fund for Nature) and the International Union for the Conservation of Nature (now the World Conservation Union). This was the World Conservation Strategy (WCS),

*A fin whale is hauled on board a factory ship. Even after world-wide protests the killing of whales continues. Conservationists think there may be only 4,000 fin whales and 1,000 blue whales left.*

and it outlined a plan for tackling the massive environmental problems facing the planet. Individual countries were encouraged to set up national conservation strategies and over 30 countries including Australia, Canada, Nepal and Costa Rica have done so.

The basis of the WCS was that conservation is linked to development. Development is the term for using the resources of the earth to live, and conservation means looking after the earth to make sure it can still provide the resources that humans need. The difficulty is finding a way to live and improve our standard of living without damaging the environment that supports us. 'Our Common Future' is the name of the report by the World Commission on Environment and Development. It was published in 1987 and again outlined ways to tackle the world's environment and development problems.

## The greener future

One thing all these reports and strategies agree on is the need for a new way of thinking about the world we live in. Many people and countries, especially those in the developed world, have viewed the earth as an unending source of resources for humans to use and as a convenient dustbin in which to dump their waste. They have shown little respect for other animals and plants on the planet. This attitude has caused many of the environmental problems facing the world today.

The WCS says 'a new ethic, embracing plants and animals, as well as people, is required for human societies to live in harmony with the natural world on which they depend for survival and well-being.' This may seem a tall order but it is beginning to happen, as humans slowly become aware of the impact they are having on the earth and the threat to their own survival as a species. It may be that we can rediscover how to live in harmony with nature. In the words of Chief Seattle, nineteenth-century chief of the Duwamish people: 'All things are connected. This we know. The earth does not belong to man. Man belongs to the earth.'

# GLOSSARY

**Acid rain** All rainfall is slightly acidic, but acid rain is moisture returning to the surface of the earth as rain, snow or mist which has become more acidic as a result of absorbing pollutants from the air.

**Adaptation** The process by which organisms change so that they can continue to survive in a changing environment.

**Algae** A group of tiny, very simple plants that have no roots, stems or leaves.

**Altitude** The height of something above sea-level.

**Arid** Dry lands where the annual rainfall is between 200 and 250 mm.

**Atmosphere** The thin layer of gases surrounding the earth, mostly made up of nitrogen and oxygen together with small amounts of other gases, water vapour and dust particles.

**Bacteria** Tiny single-celled organisms which are very simple in form. Some bacteria cause diseases in plants and animals.

**Barren** Infertile; land that cannot support the growth of crops.

**Biodegradable** Able to be broken down by the natural processes of decomposition or decay.

**Biofuel** Fuel from a living source, such as wood, animal manure and alcohol made from plants.

**Biomes** Communities of plants and animals that extend over a large area.

**Birth-rate** The number of births per 1,000 people per year.

**Cancer** A type of disease caused by the growth of abnormal cells in the body of a human or other animal.

**Cash crops** Crops grown especially to be exported in order to earn money from other countries. They are often grown to pay off debts owed by a poor country to a richer one.

**Catalytic converter** A small device fitted to the exhaust system of a petrol-engined car. It converts toxic substances such as carbon monoxide, and hydrocarbons into carbon dioxide and water.

**CFCs (chlorofluorocarbons)** A group of chemicals that damage the ozone layer. They are used in fridges and freezers, in the manufacture of polystyrene foam, and in some aerosol sprays.

**Climate** The average weather conditions of a place or region over a long period of time.

**Commodities** The name given to crops and other goods that are traded on the international market.

**Coniferous** Trees that bear cones, including pines, firs, spruces, cedars, larches and cypresses. Most are evergreen.

**Conservation** The protection and careful use of the resources of the earth so as not to damage the environment.

**Contaminate** To pollute or make impure.

**Continental shelf** The ledge of land that juts out around the edges of continents.

**Death-rate** The number of deaths per 1,000 people per year.

**Debt crisis** A situation, which has built up over the last 20 years, in which developing countries that have borrowed money from developed nations cannot afford to pay the interest on the loans or repay the loans themselves.

**Deciduous** Trees that lose their leaves at the end of the growing season.

**Deforestation** Clearing large areas of forest without replacing the trees with new ones.

Desertification The process by which land becomes desert, mainly because of overcultivation, overgrazing or deforestation.

**Developed countries** Those countries that earn most of their money through industry. They include the USA, Canada, the countries of Europe, Australia, New Zealand and Japan. They are also sometimes known as 'industrialized' countries.

**Developing countries** The poorer countries of the world, which are far less industrialized than the developed countries. Most developing nations are in Africa, Asia and Latin America.

**Dioxins** A group of chemicals that include some of the most poisonous chemicals known.

**Domestication** The process by which wild plants or animals are brought into use by humans for agricultural purposes.

**Ecological balance** The stable state in which natural communities of plants and animals exist. The balance is maintained by adaptation of the species, competition between individual organisms and among species, and other interactions between members of the communities and their environment.

**Ecology** The study of the relationship between living things and their environment.

**Ecosystem** A community of organisms that interact with each other and the environment in which they live, for example a forest or a pond.

**Erosion** The wearing away of the land by the rain, rivers, ice or wind.

**Estuary** Where a river widens and flows into the sea.

**Evergreen** Trees that keep their foliage all through the year.

**Evolution** The slow process of change in the characteristics of organisms from one generation to the next.

**Extinction** When a species of plant or animal dies out completely.

**Fallow** A word describing land that is left uncultivated for a period before it is used again.

**Famine** When people in a region go hungry and may eventually starve because supplies of food are short.

**Fertile** A word for soil that is good for growing plants.

**Fertilizers** Natural or artificial substances added to soil to improve its ability to support crops.

**Food chain** A chain of living things along which energy is passed as food. A simple example is: grass is eaten by sheep, which are eaten by humans.

**Fossil fuels** Fuels that were formed millions of years ago by the squeezing of organic (once-living) matter deep underground. Coal, oil and natural gas are fossil fuels.

**Global warming** The increase in the earth's temperature caused by the build-up of greenhouse gases in the atmosphere.

**Greenhouse effect** The process by which the earth's atmosphere allows light from the sun to pass through but prevents heat from escaping into space.

**Groundwater** Fresh water that is under the ground, contained within the rocks and soil.

**Habitat** An area, such as a forest or lake, in which plants and animals live.

**Hardwood** The wood of a broadleaved tree, such as oak, beech, mahogany or teak.

**Heavy metals** Certain metals, such as cadmium and mercury, that are poisonous. They are normally stable in the soil but are made unstable by acid rain and can then find their way into the food chain.

**Hydro-electricity** Electricity generated when flowing water turns a turbine, usually in a dam.

**Invertebrates** Animals that do not have a backbone.

**Irrigation** Supplying crop plants with water via channels or pipes in order to help them grow.

**Latitude** The distance of a place north or south of the Equator, measured as an angle from the centre of the earth.

**Longitude** The distance of a place east or west of the prime meridian (0°) – an imaginary line from the North Pole to the South Pole that passes through Greenwich, in London.

**Mammals** Warm-blooded animals that feed their young on milk produced by the mother.

**Migration** The movement of people or other animals from one area to another.

**Natural selection** The process by which the characteristics of an organism which help it to survive and multiply in its environment are passed on to its offspring.

**Niche** The place of an organism in an ecosystem – where it lives, what it eats, what it is eaten by, and so on.

**Nomads** People, normally livestock herders, who do not settle in one place but move frequently in search of new grazing for their herds.

**Nuclear power station** A power station in which electricity is made from the decay of radioactive 'fuel', such as uranium.

**Organic farming** Farming that does not use artificial fertilizers or pesticides. The soil may be kept fertile by changing regularly the way in which it is used – crop growing, livestock grazing, etc.

**Nutrients** Substances, including water and oxygen, that are taken in by a living organism to enable it to grow and repair itself.

**Oxygen** A gas that makes up 21 per cent of the air we breathe. It is essential for life.

**Ozone** A form of oxygen. At the surface of the earth it is poisonous to plants and animals, but high in the atmosphere it forms a protective layer that prevents too much ultraviolet radiation reaching the earth.

**Ozone layer** A thin layer of ozone gas in the upper atmosphere that filters out some of the sun's harmful ultraviolet radiation.

**Particulates** Tiny, often invisible particles of fossil fuel which float in the air when the fuel is not fully burnt.

**PCBs (polychlorinated biphenyls)** A group of highly poisonous chemicals. They are used for cleaning machinery, tanning leather and for other industrial purposes.

**Pesticides** Chemicals used for killing plants or animals that attack crops.

**pH** A measurement of acidity. pH7 is neutral (neither acid nor alkaline), below 7 is acid, and above 7 is alkaline.

**Phosphates** Chemicals used in fertilizers, some washing powders and other substances.

**Photosynthesis** The process by which green plants convert water and carbon dioxide into stored chemical energy using the energy of sunlight. Oxygen is given off in the process.

**Plankton** Tiny plants and animals that drift in the water of lakes, rivers and the sea. Many fish, and even huge whales, depend on plankton for food.

**Pollution** The release of materials into the air, water or land that may upset the ecological balance.

**Population** The number of things that live in a specific place; for example, the number of people living in a city, an area, a country or the world.

**Radioactive** A word to describe a material that gives out dangerous rays, or radiation, when it breaks down or decays.

**Rainforest** An area of dense tropical forest.

**Recycling** Processing waste products so that they can be used again.

**Renewable energy** Sources of energy that do not use up resources which cannot be replaced.

**Resource** Anything that is useful to living animals and plants.

**Savannah** A region of tropical grassland, often with scattered trees and bushes. The largest areas of savannah are in Africa and South America.

**Sewage** A mixture of water and waste materials from homes and industry that is carried in pipes called sewers.

**Shanty towns** Slum settlements that are built by poor people around the edges of many cities in developing countries.

**Softwood** The wood of a coniferous tree.

**Species** A distinct group of plants or animals that are able to breed among themselves but not with members of any other group.

**Supertanker** A very large, fast tanker ship that can carry more than 75,000 tonnes of oil.

**Substainable development** Economic development and activity that uses the resources available but does not harm them.

**Temperate** A word describing the mild types of climate found in parts of the world between the tropics and the polar regions.

**Terms of trade** The level at which prices are fixed for goods that are traded between countries.

**Toxic** Poisonous.

**Tropical** A word describing the hot, wet climate in the parts of the world between the tropics, on either side of the Equator.

**Turbine** A machine in which the energy of moving water, steam or air causes a blade to spin, usually to generate electricity.

**Ultraviolet radiation** Invisible light from the sun that can damage plants and animals if they are exposed to too much of it.

**Urbanization** An increase in the proportion of a country's population that lives in towns and cities.

**Water cycle** The circulation of the earth's water, in which it evaporates from the sea, lakes and rivers to the air, and turns back to a liquid to fall as rain or snow.

**Water table** The level of groundwater beneath the earth's surface.

**Water vapour** Tiny droplets of water suspended in the air.

# FURTHER READING

*Acid Rain* by J. McCormack
  (Franklin Watts, 1986)
*Blueprint for a Green Planet* by H. Girardet and
  J. Seymour (Dorling Kindersley, 1988)
*The Climate Crisis - Greenhouse Effect
  and Ozone Layer* by J. Beckdale
  (Franklin Watts,1989)
*Close to Extinction* by J. Burton
  (Franklin Watts, 1989)
*The 'Conserving Our World'* series
  (Wayland,1989/90)
*Defeating the Deserts* by L. Williams
  (Evans, 1989)
*The Gaia Atlas of Planet Management*
  edited by N. Myers (Pan, 1985)
*The Global Environment* by S. Sterling and
  S. Lyle (Longman, 1991)

*In the Rainforest* by C. Caufield
  (Heinemann,1985)
*Life on Earth* by D. Attenborough
  (Collins,1979)
The 'Save Our World' series: *This Fragile Earth,
  Water for Life, Wildlife in Danger* and *World Resources*
  (Simon & Schuster, 1990/91)
*The State of the Earth* edited by J. Seager
  (Unwin Hyman, 1990)
*Turning the Tide* by D. Bellamy and B. Quayle
  (Collins, 1986)
*The WWF Environment Handbook* by M. Carwardine
  (Macdonald Optima, 1990)
*Vanishing Habitats* by M. Bright
  (Franklin Watts, 1989)
*The Young Person's Guide to Saving the Planet*
  by D. Silver and B. Vallely (Virago, 1989)

# USEFUL ADDRESSES

## Australia
Australian Conservation Foundation,
  34 Gore Street,Fitzroy, Vic 3065
Friends of the Earth, 222 Brunswick Street,
  Fitzroy, Vic 3065
Greenpeace, 155 Pirie Street, Adelaide, SA 5000
Wilderness Society, 130 Davey Street,
  Hobart, Tas 7000

## Britain
Council for Environmental Education,
  University of Reading,
  London Road, Reading, Berks RG1 5AQ
Friends of the Earth, 26-28 Underwood Street,
  London N1 7JQ
Greenpeace, 30-31 Islington Green,
  London N1 8XE
International Centre for Conservation Education,
  Greenfield House, Guiting Power,
  Cheltenham, Glos GL54 5TZ
National Centre for Alternative Technology,
  Llwygwern Quarry, Machynlleth,
  Powys SY20 9AZ
National Society for Clean Air, 136 North Street,
  Brighton BN1 1RG
Oxfam, 274 Banbury Road, Oxford OX2 7DZ
Population Concern, 231 Tottenham Court Road,
  London W1P 9AE
Soil Association, 86-88 Colston Street,
  Bristol BS1 5BB
WATCH, The Green, Witham Park,
  Lincoln LN5 7JR
World Wide Fund for Nature, Panda House,
  Weyside Park, Godalming, Surrey GU7 1XR

## Canada
Ecology Action Center, 1657 Barrington Street,
  Suite 520, Halifax, Nova Scotia B3J 2A1
Friends of the Earth, 251 Laurier Avenue West,
  Suite 701, Ottawa, Ontario K1P 5J6
Greenpeace 427 Bloor Street West,
  Toronto, Ontario M5S 1X7
Pollution Probe, 12 Madison Avenue,
  Toronto, Ontario M5R 2S1

World Wide Fund for Nature,
  60 St Clair Avenue East, Suite 201, Toronto,
  Ontario M4T 1N5

## International
Greenpeace International, Keizersgracht 176,
  1016 DW Amsterdam, The Netherlands
United Nations Environment Programme (UNEP)
  PO Box 30552, Nairobi, Kenya
World Wide Fund for Nature (International),
  Information and Education Division,
  1196 Gland, Switzerland

## New Zealand
Environment and Conservation
  Organizations of New Zealand Inc
  (ECO), PO Box 11057 Wellington
Friends of the Earth, PO Box 39/065,
  Auckland West
Greenpeace, Private Bag, Wellsley Street,
  Auckland
World Wide Fund for Nature,
  Box 6237, Wellington

## USA
Earth Island Institute, 300 Broadway, Suite 28,
  San Francisco CA 94133-9905
Environmental Defense Fund,
  1616 P Street NW Suite 150,
  Washington DC 20036
Friends of the Earth, 530 7th Street SE
  Washington DC 20003 and 1045
  Sansome Street, San Francisco CA 94111
Greenpeace, 1611 Connecticut Avenue
  NW, Washington DC 20009
National Audubon Society, 950 Third Avenue,
  New York NY 10022
National Campaign Against Toxic Hazards,
  2000 P Street NW, Washington DC 20009
National Wildlife Federation,
  1412 16th Street NW,
  Washington DC 20036
Sierra Club, 330 Pennsylvania Avenue NW,
  Washington DC 20008

# INDEX